The End of Innocence

c.1

The End of Innocence

a memoir

By Chastity Bono
With Michele Kort

Advocate
BOOKS

A NOTE TO READERS

TO PROTECT THE PRIVACY OF CERTAIN INDIVIDUALS,
SOME NAMES HAVE BEEN CHANGED.

MANUFACTURED IN THE UNITED STATES OF AMERICA.

THIS ORIGINAL BOOK IS PUBLISHED BY
ADVOCATE BOOKS, AN IMPRINT OF ALYSON PUBLICATIONS,
P.O. BOX 4371, LOS ANGELES, CA 90078-4371.
DISTRIBUTION IN THE UNITED KINGDOM BY
TURNAROUND PUBLISHER SERVICES LTD.,
UNIT 3, OLYMPIA TRADING ESTATE, COBURG ROAD, WOOD GREEN,
LONDON N22 6TZ ENGLAND.

FIRST EDITION: MAY 2002

02 03 04 05 06 ✳ 10 9 8 7 6 5 4 3 2 1

ISBN 1-55583-620-8

LIBRARY OF CONGRESS CATALOGING-IN-PUBLICATION DATA
BONO, CHASTITY.
    THE END OF INNOCENCE : A MEMOIR / BY CHASTITY BONO WITH
MICHELE KORT.—1ST ED.
    ISBN 1-55583-620-8 (HARDCOVER)
    1. BONO, CHASTITY. 2. LESBIANS—UNITED STATES—BIOGRAPHY.
I. KORT, MICHELE. II. TITLE.
HQ75.4.B65 A3 2002
305.48'9664'092—DC21   2002002186

Dedicated in loving memory to Joan

Prologue

1982: I'm sitting in a Manhattan movie theater, close to Columbus Circle, watching *Personal Best*. I'm a thirteen-year-old punk tomboy with long blond hair that's short and spiky on top (I'll soon cut the rest of it as well), and I often wear a black leather Harley Davidson motorcycle jacket. I'm attending junior high school in New York City while my mom's performing in *Come Back to the 5 and Dime, Jimmy Dean, Jimmy Dean* on Broadway. She's flown out my best friend Gina for my birthday, and I've chosen this film because I love sports. Little do I know it will forever change the way I see myself.

In the movie, Mariel Hemingway and Patrice Donnelly play beautiful young track stars who have a passionate affair. They arm wrestle, they kiss, they make love. As I watch them, I find myself identifying with their characters. I'm athletic, just like them. But more importantly, I too am attracted to women. I'm excited by these feelings, not scared. I've never been interested in boys and have always felt different from other girls. Now everything has crystallized and makes sense to me; I finally understand myself.

A few months later my mom is throwing a Christmas party at our house in Los Angeles. Upstairs in her bedroom with a bunch of friends, I'm sitting in front of a big-screen TV, all of us watching an HBO special Mom recently taped. Everyone is enthralled with the show, which isn't unexpected. Wherever my mom is—even if it's just on TV—she draws all the attention in a room. She doesn't even try to; it's just the screwed-up fascination with celebrity in our society. I've grown up with this phenomenon, so it's no big deal.

My attention, though, is drawn to the doorway, where someone has just called out my name. "Hi, Chas," says Joan, a friend of my mom's whom I've known since I was eleven. I have pictures of Joan and me back then, sitting on a fence by our house in Aspen. Back then I didn't pay her any particular notice. But now I'm thirteen, I've just discovered my sexual orientation, and as I turn to greet her everything in the room loses focus except for Joan. Her presence radiates, so bright and alive. I'm seeing her for the very first time, really *seeing* her. Even with all these people around us, I feel alone with her. I've heard my mom describe the first time she saw my dad in similar terms; I guess it could be a genetic trait.

Joan Leslie Stephens is thirty-six but looks younger. She's five foot ten with wavy, past-her-shoulders-length blond hair, striking long legs, and very feminine curves. She's showing those curves off to excellent effect in a black leather miniskirt, black pumps, fishnet stockings, and a low-cut red silk blouse. Joan never misses an opportunity to show off her 36-C cleavage, but in my innocence I'm more focused on her bright, sparkling blue eyes. It's as if Joan's smile comes from those brilliant eyes.

"H-h-hi, Joan," I barely manage, dazed by the tide of feeling that has swept over me.

"Chas, this is Connie," Joan says, introducing her date. Joan is very open about her relationships with women.

"Nice to meet you," I lie.

"Well, we're going to go find your mom. See ya later," says Joan, and she's gone.

In these brief moments, everything in the world has changed for me. I scout the room, wondering if anyone has noticed that my face is as red as Joan's blouse. To my amazement, everyone's eyes are glued to the TV. Hasn't anyone noticed the glow Joan brought into the room? Hasn't anyone realized, with those two lovely words— "Hi, Chas"—that I have become an adult? I guess everyone's too engrossed in my mom to take heed of my shocking transformation.

I catch my breath before going to look for Joan. After what feels like hours, but is probably only thirty seconds, I find her in the kitchen, drinking a beer. *My God, she's gorgeous,* I think. *Why haven't I ever seen her in this way before? Oh, the wasted years!*

In our vast kitchen, I position myself near the stove, where I can watch her unobserved. She must sense my gaze, as she periodically glances over at me and smiles. I look down when our eyes meet, engrossed in my sneakers, trying to come up with an excuse to talk to her.

"How's school going, Chas?" She has suddenly materialized before me.

"OK," I say, looking up from my shoelaces. Standing

so close to her, inhaling the sweet scent of the perfume that always shadows her, I am intoxicated.

"So, do you have a boyfriend yet?"

"No," I answer, a bit insulted.

"No time for boys, huh?" She smirks slightly. Her gaydar—that unerring sense that allows a gay person to spot another—is clearly in working order.

"Absolutely not," I say emphatically. "I still have a few more basketball games to play—we might make the city playoffs—and I'm already training for softball." I'm desperately trying to impress her with my athletic ability.

"That's great, Chas," Joan says, her smirk blossoming into a full grin.

"I'm also writing a screenplay about a college girls basketball team," I add, trying to sound intellectual as well as sporty.

"I didn't know you were interested in writing."

"Oh, yeah," I brag, "ever since I saw *Personal Best*. Did you see it?"

"Yes." She gives me a knowing look.

"Well, I really liked it—a lot!" I announce. "And since it seemed to do pretty well, I started my own screenplay. You know, kind of a basketball version."

Joan's expression turns serious yet tender. "Chas," she says gently, "Connie and I are getting ready to go home, but I'm really glad we got a chance to catch up. Look, even though I'm about a million years older than you"—it's actually twenty-three years, but who's counting?—"if you ever need someone to talk with...about anything...I'm a really good listener."

With that, she kisses me on the cheek and disappears into the crowd to find Connie. In the coming months, I *will* call Joan to talk. I'll ask her out to eat, or to the movies, or to come over and visit. She's no longer just my mom's friend: She's mine now too. Along with wanting Joan's friendship, I gradually imagine something more. I already feel the makings of a serious crush—a crush that will never really go away.

ONE

It was a clear and breezy night in August 1987, and I was brimming with excitement. I had just graduated from high school and was about to attend my first lesbian party. Joan's friend Sandy was throwing it, and Joan invited me to meet her and her girlfriend Leslie there. Now that I was of age, the idea of being in a room full of gay women was almost too wonderful to imagine.

In preparation for the big event, I spent hours blow-drying my long hair and choosing my outfit: black Levi's 501s, a blue button-down shirt, a black blazer, and black lizard-skin cowboy boots. I desperately wanted to look like the quintessential well-dressed young gay woman.

With my newly obtained driver's license in hand (my dad had just taught me to drive), I climbed into my rental car and headed through the hills from Benedict Canyon to Studio City. When I arrived at the party, my pounding heart and fluttering stomach were soothed when I spotted Joan's 1973 Porsche Carrera in the driveway. Already a classic in '87, it was the only Porsche I'd seen in such an intense shade of blue, so I knew for certain Joan had arrived.

A lot had happened to me since that hormone-awakening Christmas party when I was thirteen. That summer, after I turned fourteen, I kissed a girl for the first time—a classmate of mine at the Lee Strasberg Theatre Institute in West Hollywood. I had started taking acting and singing classes there in eighth grade, since I hated the fancy private Curtis School I attended. I found the kids at Curtis to be superficial, and I didn't make any friends there at all. My mom saw how depressed I was and thought I'd be more comfortable in a creative environment. She was absolutely right. I also enrolled in the summer program at Strasberg, where I made a lot of friends (including my kissing cohort) and discovered a love of acting.

That led me to audition for, and get accepted at, the High School for Performing Arts in New York City—the school depicted in the movie *Fame*. At first the other students didn't know what to make of me, because of my famous parents. At Strasberg a lot of the kids had celebrity parents, so mine were no big deal, but Performing Arts is a public school, attended by a diverse group of kids, and my classmates really gawked over me. That blew me away. It was the first time in my life that I realized people wanted to be around me—or, conversely, resented me—simply because I was the daughter of Sonny and Cher. There were even crazy rumors flying around that the only reason I got in was because my mom had bought the school new video equipment. I really felt out of place for a while, but after a month or two the novelty wore off, and I became just another freshman. I spent four great years there, majoring in drama.

In the open, artistic environment of Performing Arts, it was safe for me to be gay. I hadn't yet come out to my parents, but I could be honest with my friends, who were completely accepting—a luxury few gay kids enjoy. Even after my first kiss, I figured I'd probably remain a virgin until I was twenty-one, since that's when I could legally go to bars in New York City. I assumed gay people only met each other in bars. Thankfully, I was wrong.

In fact, sex wasn't that hard to come by in high school; it was more available than I even took advantage of. Since I was the only out lesbian at school, girls who wanted to experiment with their sexuality often hit on me, making me feel like the resident lab rat. But the girls I had crushes on— typically the straight, feminine-looking girls—usually weren't interested in me, while the experimenters were often good friends of mine whom I didn't want as lovers. Finding love was much more of a challenge than going to bed with someone.

In my junior year, I fell particularly hard for a girl named Julie, who was troubled by her sexual orientation. We had an on-again, off-again relationship for the next year and a half, usually dictated by her anxieties.

During one of my off-again periods with Julie, I had a brief fling with a fellow drama student. It was the summer before my senior year, and Beth was an uptight, unremarkable-looking girl with short, curly hair who had been in my circle of friends. After seeing a film together one night, we started flirting and ended up sleeping together. I didn't have strong feelings for her—actually, the only thing I found attractive about her was the smell of the Agree conditioner she used on her hair!—but I was looking for someone to take my mind off Julie. When we returned to school in the fall, Beth started telling people that I was her girlfriend, and that made me nervous, so I broke up with her. She was hurt, and unfortunately this coincided with us being cast as two of the three witches in *Macbeth*. It was a riot, actually: Beth was having temper tantrums and walking out of rehearsals, which made for a very tense set. The poor third witch—a very nice straight girl—was unknowingly caught right in the middle of our vicious young dyke drama. Talk about double bubble, toil, and trouble.

During my years in Manhattan, Joan remained a constant in my life, as both a friend and confidante. We'd talk on the phone often and hang out together during the summers I spent in Los Angeles. It wasn't really strange that I wanted to hang out with someone so much older. Having been on the road with my mom, I was used to being around adults. In many ways I was a lot more mature than your average teenager.

My mom wasn't always around, since she was working, so Joan sort of filled in that gap. She always took the time and effort to make me feel loved and appreciated. My mom was career-driven, and for good reason: She had two kids and other family members to support. But at the time I wasn't able to rationalize that my mom was thinking of me and my needs by working: I just focused on the fact that I wasn't getting enough attention, and I often felt lonely or abandoned. When I spent time with Joan, I felt like the center of attention, even when there were a lot of other people around her. She had a gift for making people feel special.

Joan didn't have my mom's sort of drive, and she was very old-fashioned in certain ways. She was perfectly content to be more of a homebody while the feminist movement passed her by. There was something very simplistic about her; she really focused on enjoying life. It might have been easy for some people to look down on her for not having grander ambitions, but I admired it. Most people drive themselves crazy over how they're going to make their mark and feel complete and worthwhile. There's a great side to being career-driven, but it can also be torturous. Joan's main goal in life was just to have love, give love, and create a loving, comfortable atmosphere around her—and in all of that she succeeded very well.

Joan knew I was gay, of course—she'd figured that one out pretty quickly—and because she was older and more experienced, she gave me advice my peers couldn't begin to offer. (I can even remember her girlfriend Leslie taking me aside once, when I was about fifteen, and telling me what to do sexually with a girl, because I was totally naive.) Unlike the other adults in my life, Joan was nonjudgmental about issues relating to gender and sexuality. In comparison, during my freshman year at Performing Arts, I lived with acting teacher Anna Strasberg and her two sons, and although Anna realized I was gay, she still criticized me for not dressing more femininely or for having friends whose hair was too short. Joan, on the other hand, was always totally accepting of who I was and who I wanted to be.

Joan had had quite a tough childhood herself, with parents who didn't give her nearly the acceptance and love she needed. Maybe that's one reason she was so understanding and why maintaining a nurturing home was so primary to her. An only child born in a Nebraska farm town, she moved with her mother to Los Angeles when she was about six years old. Her biker father had left them, but her mom remarried, and Joan's stepfather, a truck driver, turned out to be both sexually suggestive to her and physically abusive. Once he had even split open Joan's lip, which left her with a small scar. She hated him and was furious with her mother for not doing anything about his abuse. She couldn't wait to move out of the house, marking the days until her eighteenth birthday on a calendar. One day her stepfather asked what the marks meant, and she answered, "They're the days until my eighteenth birthday, when I'll be free to leave." He said, "You don't have to wait," and packed her bags for her. At age seventeen she was on her own.

Joan grew up expecting she'd get married and have a family. She told me she had lost her virginity to her boyfriend, Jim, in twelfth grade and had thought she would marry him, but they split up after he was drafted to fight in Vietnam. After Joan left home, she became a go-go dancer—performing in clubs on a stage or platform, fully clothed—and later she danced in Vegas as a showgirl, also fully clothed. These were the only jobs she'd ever have. She tried to reestablish some sort of connection with her real father, but her mother freaked out when she found out, still mad at her ex for having left and jealous of Joan for having regained his favor. Her mom's reaction was so strong and bitter that it tore them apart and Joan never saw her mother again.

✳

Sandy's party was held at her tastefully decorated three-bedroom house in the Valley. Most of the women were in their mid thirties—professionals wearing pantsuits. No one looked terribly glamorous or exciting. I was hoping to find some cute women in their twenties, but they just weren't there.

As I entered the house I spotted Leslie, the short, redheaded real estate agent Joan had dated regularly for years. I liked her a lot; she was fun to hang out with, friendly, and good-natured.

"Hey, Les, what's going on?" I greeted her with a hug and some slaps on the back.

"Nothing much," Leslie smiled. "Yourself?"

"Just getting ready to head back to New York and start NYU."

"That's great," she remarked, looking distracted. She probably wasn't particularly interested in a teenager about to go off to college.

I headed for the bar, where I grabbed a beer and scanned the room for someone I might find attractive. If I saw her, I promised myself, I'd try to muster up the courage to talk to her. Since I was ten to twenty years younger than everyone else, I figured I was at both an advantage and disadvantage: I would at least get some attention because of my youth, but then again I'd be less likely to find such older women to be my type. In fact, no one caught my eye—until I saw Joan in a sleeveless summer dress, sparkling like a Christmas tree in August.

The other guests seemed like obstacles in my path as

I dodged them to get closer to her. Near the kitchen I finally reached my target, sneaking up from behind and wrapping my arms around her, burying my face in her fragrant-smelling hair.

"Hi, pretty lady," I whispered boldly in Joan's ear. Although I was just eighteen, I was surprisingly gutsy with women who interested me—more so than I would be later in life. Even with someone as unlikely as Joan, I wasn't afraid to flirt a little and see what kind of response I'd get. I wasn't making an overt pass, but I was pushing the envelope a bit.

Recognizing my voice immediately, Joan turned to give me a hug and kiss. "Hi, baby," she said. "I'm so glad you came."

"Me too."

"You look great," she said, flashing me a warm smile.

"Thanks." I was almost blushing now. "You're not looking too bad yourself."

Despite our age difference, and even though I was still in my teens, there had always been a subtle sexual charge between us, ever since I'd realized I was gay. I knew people often perceived Joan's outgoing, friendly personality as flirtation, but I felt she was somehow more serious with me.

"I want to introduce you to Sandy." Joan took my hand and pulled me toward a dark-haired woman in an attractive suit. "Sandy, this is my friend Chas. Chas, meet Sandy, the hostess of this fabulous soiree."

"Nice to meet you," Sandy and I chimed in unison.

"Now, if you'll excuse us," Joan said, politely pulling me away, "I want to take Chas around to mingle."

As we wandered through the party, Joan confessed why Les had acted rather distracted and cool: Joan's other longtime girlfriend, Connie, was also at the party. I wasn't as fond of Connie, a doctor with no bedside manner, let alone personality. Both she and Leslie knew about each other and hated that Joan wouldn't pick one of them to date exclusively, but apparently they didn't hate it enough to stop seeing Joan. This night they spent much of the evening staring each other down from across the room, and in their silent battle they seemed to have forgotten that Joan was even there.

"Since they're ignoring me, will you be my date tonight?" Joan asked me teasingly.

"If I were your date," I told her, "I wouldn't leave your side."

Maybe it was the beer. Maybe it was the fact that I'd had a few years of practice at being gay. I wasn't being coy at all about the vibe between us. But then she threw me a curve ball.

"Anyone you'd like me to introduce you to? Anyone you'd like to get to know a little better?" Joan asked with a devilish glint in her eye.

"I'm insulted," I said, in mock horror. "I thought you were my date tonight, and now you're trying to pawn me off!"

"I just thought you might want to meet a nice woman born in the same decade as you."

I hadn't been paying attention to our age difference. Obviously, Joan had.

"Joan," I locked eyes with her, all business, "there's no one else I'd rather spend the evening with. You are the most beautiful, dazzling woman here. I'd be honored to be your escort, while your date and your other woman waste the evening marking their territory."

"You're absolutely right...about the beautiful and dazzling part," she giggled. "As for Leslie and Connie, they can spend the night pissing on the furniture like a couple of pit bulls. We won't let them spoil our evening. You and I, my darling, are going to have some fun."

And we did. We talked and laughed, drank way too much, and openly flirted with each other while the battling girlfriends didn't even notice. Toward the end of the party, Joan and I danced together oh-so suggestively, in a way I never had before. I was lost in a haze of liquor, possibility, and her.

By the time the party was winding down and it was time to go, I was too drunk to drive. With my license just days old, the last thing I needed was a DUI. Since Joan's house was just a few blocks away, she invited me to sleep over in her guest room. Leslie, who finally joined us after Connie left, offered to drive my car to Joan's while I rode over with Joan in her Porsche.

Before Joan started the engine, she told me she felt cold, which wasn't surprising, considering the lightweight dress she had on. So I slid my arms around her and gently rubbed my hands over her goose bumps. "Thanks, baby," she said, turning the key in the ignition. "Let's wait here until the heat kicks in."

Of course, it already had for me. After the evening we had shared, being in the car alone with Joan and holding her close, I was on fire. She hugged me to get warm—supposedly—and her flawless face snuggled into my neck. Then as I turned my own face toward hers, she lifted her head slightly. Before I knew what was happening, my lips were brushing against hers. At first it was tentative, but then we were kissing deeply and passionately. I'd wanted this to happen since the night she'd appeared in my mom's bedroom doorway five years before. Now I was being carried away, transported, living out my most treasured secret fantasy.

Soon my hand strayed to her breast, which somehow broke the spell. "I think we need to get going," Joan said, flustered. "Les will wonder why we aren't home yet." Without a word, she pulled out into the street and we drove in complete silence, holding hands. After three blocks I couldn't stand it any longer.

"Joan, pull over," I demanded.

Without question she did as told, and we picked up where we had left off. I could have spent all night kissing her, but this time it was me who pulled back to regain composure. "I think we'd better get home before Les comes looking for us," I said sensibly through the alcohol and lust.

This time we only made it two blocks before Joan abruptly pulled the car over to the curb again. She almost pushed herself on top of me, kissing me with complete abandon and running her hands over my body.

But our third bout didn't last long, as light suddenly flooded the inside of the car. *Busted.* "Oh, fuck," Joan whispered, as we yanked ourselves apart. "It's Leslie."

Leslie had pulled up behind us and turned on her brights at the most inopportune moment possible.

"Follow me back to the house!" Les yelled, taking off.

We dutifully drove after her, and as we pulled into Joan's driveway, I panicked. "Oh, God, Joan, what are we going to do?" I was practically shaking. "Les is going to kill me! Fuck! Fuck! Fuck! I can't believe she busted us! Let's just keep driving. I can't deal with this!"

Joan placed a hand on my shoulder in a feeble attempt to calm me down. "Don't worry. I'll deal with her."

Leslie had stepped out of my rental car and was now pacing furiously. "Goddamn it, Joan, I can't fucking believe you! It was bad enough that I had to spend the whole night staring at Connie, but then you go sink your teeth into Chas! Christ, Joan, she's only eighteen fucking years old!"

Clearly, Les assumed I was the innocent party. I certainly wasn't going to tell her otherwise.

Somehow through all the yelling and fighting, we made it into Joan's house.

"You know we don't have an exclusive relationship," Joan told Leslie sternly.

"But are you so fucking desperate that you would stoop to fucking around with a baby?" Leslie screamed.

"Fuck you." Without another word, Joan stormed off to her bedroom. Leslie and I heard the loud click of the lock behind her.

"I'm really sorry about this," I told Leslie, trying to sound as sincere and sober as possible. But we were both very, very drunk.

"I'm not mad at you, Chas," Les said, heading out to Joan's backyard. I followed and offered her a cigarette. We sat outside a while, having a smoke together, but nothing could soothe her or calm my own nerves. When she ranted loudly about Joan being a slut, I suggested she turn down the volume so the neighbors wouldn't complain, but she was very wound up.

"I'm Irish—I've got a hot temper, OK?" she shouted as we headed back inside.

Suddenly Joan's bedroom door flew open, and she poked her head out. "Will you both leave my house? Now!"

Then she slammed the door and locked herself in again.

I started to panic. "I'm still too drunk to drive home," I told Leslie.

"You can crash on my couch."

"Even after what happened tonight?"

"I told you, I'm not mad at you. Come on, kid, let's get out of here."

So that night I experienced some rather significant firsts: I attended my first lesbian party. I kissed Joan for the first time. And now I *really* knew what dyke drama was all about.

✳

Considering the fact that Joan was originally my mom's friend, you might wonder how my mother felt about our close friendship.

Her feelings were mixed. On the one hand, I think she appreciated the fact that I had an older confidante whom she knew and liked. But it also disturbed her that this confidante happened to be one of her only lesbian friends. I wasn't open with my mom then—she wouldn't figure out about my sexuality until I was a freshman in college—but she had long been concerned that I was gay. I'd given her some strong hints in that direction early on, since I always wanted to be a male character (like Dracula or Wolf Man) for Halloween. I gave her more reason for concern when I was eleven and my mom, her boyfriend, her manager, and I were in a Paris hotel room and decided to dress up for fun and take Polaroids of each other. I dressed up as a leather-jacketed biker, my hair slicked back in a pompadour, a switchblade from my pocketknife collection in my hand, and an unlit cigarette dangling out of my mouth. My mom later told me that the moment I came into her room in Paris wearing that outfit, she felt really scared about me.

There's a long, complicated family history behind my mom's friendship with Joan. It starts back a generation with Scotti, a gay woman who became romantically involved with a good friend of my grandmother's on my mother's side. A petite, almost elfin woman of half-Hawaiian (she grew up in the islands), half-Scottish parentage, Scotti was a classic old-school dyke, with her hair greased back in a DA. She wasn't conventionally attractive, but she was cute and debonair in a butch way, and in her younger days she often ended up with attractive straight women who would inevitably break her heart. My grandmother never liked her very much. I don't think she ever understood why her friend—one of Scotti's straight conquests—had gotten involved in a lesbian relationship. Rather than disliking her friend, however, my grandmother chose to dislike Scotti.

My mother, though—who was thirteen or fourteen at the time—gravitated to Scotti. She told me she liked how Scotti listened to her. She was fun to be around and didn't treat my mom like a kid. In fact, my mom enjoyed being around Scotti for many of the same reasons I later appreciated Joan. Of course, my grandmother wasn't thrilled that her adolescent daughter hung around with a lesbian.

It's ironic that when I was in high school, my mom became similarly worried about Joan and me. At one point she asked me point-blank, "Are you gay or just pro gay?" I told her I just enjoyed being around Joan, that I had a good time with her. My mom then insisted I go to her psychiatrist, who also asked if I was gay. I lied and said I wasn't. I guess she believed me and reported that to my mom. Relieved, my mom let the subject slide after that. The shrink probably told her that if she tried to restrict me from seeing Joan, it would make me want to be around her even more.

A couple of years after she met Scotti, my mom became best friends with a girl named Della, whom she'd known since the fourth grade. Della was basically a straight girl with a wild, experimental streak. Like my mom, she loved Scotti and became friends with her as well. Now enter Joan, who was also a friend of Della's. After Joan's stepfather had kicked her out, she moved in with Della's family, and soon my mom, Della, and Joan were hanging out together.

Both Della and my mom mentioned Scotti to Joan, saying how cool she was. From their description, Joan certainly would have recognized Scotti if she ran into her—which she did one evening at a gay men's club where Joan had gone to dance. Joan loved dancing, and when she had worked as a go-go dancer it was at a straight club owned by my grandmother's brother. Joan liked to dance at gay men's bars, since she didn't have to worry about getting hit on. (Years later, Joan and my mom went together to men's bars for the same reason.) That night, however, some uptight gay guy hassled Joan about being there. Scotti, being a tough and chivalrous Navy vet, immediately went to the rescue of this attractive blond femme.

The minute she saw a five-foot-tall Hawaiian dyke coming her way, Joan knew that this was the famous Scotti. After doing Joan the favor of getting rid of the guy, Scotti spent the rest of the evening with her. Sparks flew. Even though Scotti was at least twenty years older than Joan, who was about eighteen at the time, the two of them ended up having sex that night in Scotti's car. It was Joan's first lesbian experience. Joan had always been boy-crazy and hadn't given a thought to being gay, but Scotti—who was like a small-statured man—somehow swept her off her feet. Joan and Scotti remained lovers for the next two years, living in Scotti's house in the San Fernando Valley, and then their relationship transformed into a lifelong friendship.

Meanwhile, my father had entered the picture when my mom was sixteen. She dropped out of high school and moved in with him, although they didn't get married until years later, when I was born. After a while he started getting upset about her friendship with Joan and Scotti. He didn't really want her having *any* friends, since he was very controlling at the time, but the fact that these particular friends were lesbians made them even more threatening. Mostly my dad didn't want my mom to do anything without him, and he wanted her to be working constantly. Once they became famous, the joke was that if Sonny and Cher had a gig in the San Fernando Valley, on their way home to Bel Air he'd book another gig on Mulholland Drive. In those years my mom was pretty much ruled by what my dad said, so over time she lost touch with Joan and Scotti.

Leap ahead to 1980, when my parents had been split up for about seven years and my mom was dating Les Dudek, a rock guitarist. Les mentioned something to my mom about his next-door neighbors in the Valley: Joan and Scotti. *What are the odds?* my mom thought. So the next time she spent the night at Les's, she went over and knocked on their door. Sure enough, it was her old buddies, and they rekindled their friendship as if no time had passed.

In the years since my mom had lost touch with her, Joan had gone back and forth between women and men. When she and Scotti broke up, she figured that their two years together had just been an isolated lesbian incident and that she really was straight. Her next relationship turned out to be even more unusual, though: When she was twenty, she got involved with Scotti's godson, Steve, who at the time they first connected was only fifteen or sixteen years old.

Steve's mother had been an old lover of Scotti's—Scotti had two godsons whose mothers were straight women with whom she'd had romantic relationships—and Joan had become good friends with her as well. Steve's mom actually encouraged Joan to sleep with her son, because she felt it was time he lost his virginity. She wanted his first time to be with someone she trusted and who would provide a good experience for him. It seems rather bizarre now, but I guess things were different in the late 1960s, when people had more of a free-love attitude toward sex. Joan was definitely game for such exploits, and Steve's youth didn't matter to her. She always said to me that she liked and respected young people; she appreciated how their point of view hadn't yet been tainted or jaded by society's prejudices and the hardships of life. Besides, Joan was an unbelievably free spirit, not restricted by conventional societal views.

Joan's "favor" to Steve turned into much more: She fell in love with him, and they started a relationship that lasted eight years. In the end, he broke up with her because he'd never had the chance to sow his wild oats. Joan was devastated. Steve later realized what he'd lost and wanted to get back together with her, but by then she had moved on.

Even after Joan began seeing Steve, she and Scotti continued to live together, their relationship gradually becoming more like mother (or perhaps father) and daughter. I'm sure it was difficult for Scotti when Joan got involved with Steve, but her connection with Joan remained deep and lasting. From Joan's point of view, after having had such a terrible childhood, she appreciated how well Scotti treated her both emotionally and financially.

There was another odd twist to the story: Long before meeting Joan, Scotti had gotten married to a man for the financial support he offered. She tried to make a go of the marriage but couldn't—she was such a full-on dyke—so she left him and moved to Paris for a year. During the time she was away, her husband remained desperate for them to keep the marriage together, so he made a deal with her: As long as she spent one afternoon a week with him and remained his wife, he'd continue to support her. The rest of her life remained private from him—he didn't even know she was a lesbian! She was fortunate that he had a medical condition that rendered him impotent, so she mainly supplied him with companionship during their weekly visits, and they both kept up their end of the bargain until he died in the early 1980s.

Since this arrangement had worked so well for her, Scotti suggested that Joan, too, seek out a rich man who would take care of her financial needs other than housing (Scotti owned the house they lived in). So Joan began dating a businessman from Ohio who was the uncle of one of her friends. Irving was twenty years older, married with children, and looking for a woman on the side. Joan was willing to make just such an arrangement. In return for spending a couple of weeks with him twice a year and being available for long phone conversations, Irving sent Joan a regular support check, lavished her with jewelry and designer clothing, and even bought a house in Honolulu (co-owned with Scotti's brother) where they could meet clandestinely. It's hard to understand such a setup today, but Scotti and Joan grew up in a much different era, when lesbians certainly weren't as accepted as they are today. They both expected men to take care of them, so they made that happen.

Amazingly, over the next two decades Irving believed Joan was having a monogamous relationship with him. Even when she'd invite Steve or one of her female lovers to come to Hawaii with her, Irving thought they were just friends and never suspected anything else. Although Joan had to deliver sexually to keep up her end of the bargain, she certainly wasn't interested in Irving that way. She acted so undemonstrative with him in bed, in fact, that he came to believe she was timid about sex—so he bought her a how-to sex manual. Joan and I had quite a laugh about this. Little did he know that Joan was quite a sexual adventurer—just not with him! Sex wasn't the most important part of their relationship, though: Irving, who wasn't a particularly attractive man, mostly loved having a beautiful woman on his arm to show off in places like Los Angeles, Hawaii, or Las Vegas.

✳

Now back to the aftermath of that drunken night with Joan when I was eighteen.

I was about to return to New York for college, but I had a couple of weeks left in Los Angeles, so Joan and I had a chance to be together a few more times. Even sober, we found ourselves fooling around with each other, kissing and touching. One evening we even considered sleeping together, but Leslie came over to Joan's that night to do her laundry, so nothing happened. In retrospect I realize it was a good thing, since I would have been way out of my league at that young age.

Eventually Joan and Leslie fell back into their familiar, but not particularly healthy, relationship, and my indiscretion with Joan was forgotten. I returned to New York to start the film program at NYU, and although my feelings for Joan that had been aroused lingered a while, I was ready to move on and focus on college. I was also about to meet my first serious lover.

It happened shortly after I began my freshman year. A fellow student named Amy approached me after one of my theater classes, asking if she could borrow my notes for her roommate who was ill. Amy and I became fast friends—she was the first lesbian I'd met at college—and soon after I met her roommate, Rachel. Although Rachel was involved with a woman named Donna, she and I felt an instant attraction to each other (she and Donna were about to break up). Not long after our first encounter, I made plans to meet her in San Francisco to see the Grateful Dead perform on New Year's Eve. (Rachel was a huge Deadhead and had caravanned from show to show when she was a teenager.) By the time we flew back to New York City a couple of days after the concert (the first of about fifty Dead concerts I would see with Rachel), we'd fallen head over heels in love with each other.

Rachel, who was five years older than me, was a senior in the film department at NYU. She was openly gay, outspoken, funny, an effortless straight-A student, and a talented screenwriter. She had written a play that I thought was amazing. Rachel was also beautiful—tall, thin, green-eyed, with curly blond shoulder-length hair. She had a great smile, with cute small teeth and full lips. At first I could hardly look her in the eye—I just stared at her lips, because I loved how they looked when she talked. I'd never met anyone like her. Up to that point, my sexual relationships had all been with straight girls who were experimenting. This was a woman who was close to my age and proud to be gay.

Our family backgrounds were as different as night and day. Rachel was from an upper-middle-class Jewish family on Long Island, her father a pharmacist and her mother a stay-at-home mom. They were a typical American nuclear family, except that Rachel was the black sheep among three sisters because she was artsy and a lesbian—the latter being something her parents didn't react kindly to when she told them at age nineteen.

In comparison, I'd grown up in Los Angeles with divorced show-business parents and had shuttled back and forth between their homes. We were always moving too, as my mom liked to buy and renovate houses, and there seemed to always be some sort of construction or remodeling going on. At one point she spent *years* building our Benedict Canyon house, so we lived in three or four other houses during that period. My family was a lot more chaotic than nuclear.

The contrasts between Rachel and me didn't set us apart, though. On the contrary, I was completely taken by her intelligence, beauty, and boldness. By the end of March 1988 we were living together, along with Amy.

As a result of our relationship, however, my scholastic career took a nosedive. Since Rachel was a senior, she rarely went to class; since I was in a relationship for the first time, I didn't go to class either. I wasn't enjoying being a film major anyway. I knew I should have been studying acting instead, but I was partially scared away from that by my teachers at Performing Arts. They had drilled into us the difficulty of being a working actor, saying that if we could be happy in any other career we should avoid the profession.

Even more significantly, I didn't believe I'd find parts in commercial films that would suit me. The roles I had excelled at in high school were offbeat—a witch in *Macbeth* and the rustic Peter Quince in *A Midsummer Night's Dream*. I felt I always came up short when I played a conventional female part, because my demeanor was too masculine. All I saw on screen in the late '80s were ingenues—independent films hadn't really taken off yet—and I knew I wasn't an ingenue.

So I thought I would *make* films instead and create roles I'd feel comfortable playing. When I'd gone to Europe with my friend Sheila the summer before, I'd even written down some ideas for a gay script. (It's interesting that years later I ended up working for GLAAD, advising the entertainment media on portrayals of gays and lesbians.) The problem was, once I got to NYU, I discovered I didn't like making films. I'm not a very visual person, which is clearly something you need to be when you're behind a camera.

So I wasn't motivated to stay in college, especially after Rachel graduated in June. She was twenty-three and would soon be getting a job, and I was scared of losing her. I guess I thought I made a better lover than student, so at the end of my freshman year I dropped out. My parents weren't concerned about it, since education wasn't really stressed in my family. Neither of them had graduated from high school, and they both had done well in their careers. Not having a college degree hasn't hurt or limited my life, but in retrospect I wish I hadn't dropped out.

With school over for both of us, Rachel and I decided to spend the summer of 1988 bumming around Europe and figuring out what to do with our lives. Actually, we spent much of the trip stressing out about it, talking constantly about what the hell we were going to do. The best we could come up with was the idea of moving to Los Angeles, where Rachel could get a job in film production and I could become a singer—the most logical career for me, given my family background. I didn't play an instrument yet, but I had studied singing at the Strasberg Institute. (I'd even performed with my dad one New Year's Eve, when I sang my mom's part in "I've Got You Babe" and "The Beat Goes On" at a '60s revival concert in Palm Springs.)

One warm July night in Paris—one of my favorite places—Rachel and I walked back from the Louvre to our little hotel in the Latin Quarter and stopped on one of the many bridges that cross the Seine. As we watched a painter applying brush to canvas, our conversation turned to our future careers.

"Let's open an antiques store here," I said, flashing Rachel a wide smile to let her know I was at least half kidding. After all, in Amsterdam we'd said, "Let's open a hash bar!"

"I love Paris," Rachel said, "but I wouldn't want to be so far away from my family."

"You know I'm joking," I laughed. "But we've got to figure out something, especially since you don't seem that enthused about being a production assistant."

"You're right. PAs are just glorified gofers. It's not creative enough for me. But I don't know what else I'm qualified to do with my degree."

We were silent for a while, both of us looking out at the gorgeous Paris sunset. Then I had an idea. "What if we try to do music *together*?" I asked her. I was nervous about going into music on my own, so I hoped Rachel would join me. We'd been harmonizing to songs by the Beatles and Neil Young ever since we'd met, with Rachel accompanying us on her guitar.

"I'm not a singer—what are you talking about?" She looked surprised.

"Our voices blend well together!"

"I like to *go* to concerts, not *be* the concert."

"You love music more than anyone I've ever met," I insisted. "Don't tell me you've never fantasized about being on stage. What about all those times you played air guitar with your tennis racket when you were a kid?"

Rachel laughed. "OK, I've fantasized about it, but there's a big difference between fantasy and reality."

"The only difference is having the courage to try," I said. "I've been writing songs since I was twelve. You're a great writer yourself—you could easily translate your talent for screenwriting into writing lyrics. Plus, you play guitar and piano. It would be so much fun to do this. I don't know if I could do it alone, but I know I could do it with you."

Rachel paused, and then a smile slowly crossed her face. "We do sound pretty good together."

"Yeah, we do." I could tell I was starting to reel her in. "And when we get back home, we can start trying to write and arrange songs for our voices. I have some savings— we can go out and buy some instruments and recording equipment and start making demos."

Rachel stared at the sunset for a while then turned to me. "All right," she finally agreed. "Who knows what will come out of it, but when we get back home, let's try."

That night we called our roommate Amy and asked her to be our manager. She was a logical choice, since she had excellent people skills, was a pretty good hustler, and knew a bunch of musicians. Amy was totally into the idea and immediately started acting like an uptight manager when we got back to the States, to the point of suggesting that we get fake boyfriends and stop going to gay bars. With that, the wheels were set in motion: We were ready to start a music career, and we were prepared to lock ourselves in the closet.

Of course, I didn't have any concept of how difficult the music industry would be. My parents had been popular since before I was born, so I'd never seen them struggle. I just saw their success. Clearly I had a lot to learn. But once Rachel and I made our decision on that Paris bridge, we never looked back.

TWO

That fall of 1988, Rachel and I lived together (with Amy) in the place where I'd first met her—a sixth-floor, two-story penthouse apartment on 10th and University in Manhattan, near NYU. Rachel's parents had bought it for her to live in while she was at school. I have to admit that the place was disgustingly messy, since none of us were good housekeepers. We were like college guys, real slobs, yet we entertained a lot. I think our friends liked our apartment because they never had to worry about messing anything up. Joan, though, later told me that whenever she came over, she was afraid to sit anywhere.

Rachel and I slept in the master bedroom upstairs, and the large living room downstairs was partitioned with Japanese sliding blinds, with Amy using half the space as her bedroom. Poor Amy—the downstairs also became our music studio. We bought some rudimentary equipment (a TEAC four-track porti-studio) and some instruments, and started to write songs and produce home demos. Rachel played guitar and piano, and we both sang. All we had for percussion was a drum machine, which I didn't know how to program, so I played the drum parts with my fingers as if I were typing. I even did drum fills like that. We were as raw as you could get.

A demo usually consists of about three songs, but ours included six songs that were really, really long. One of them was so long we nicknamed it "The Iliad and the Odyssey Combined." We had no clue about song structure or radio sensibility—we just wrote what was on our minds, and if we had something more to say, we added a verse.

Our songs sounded folkish, influenced by the Grateful Dead and the Beatles. As for lyrical content, they were about, well...nothing, really—at least nothing that we were actually going through. Rachel was into the poetry of how words sounded together, not what they meant. And what was there to write about? I was nineteen, Rachel was twenty-four. We hadn't lived much. We had a surprising amount of confidence, though, and we also made a great connection with Bob Weir, the guitarist for the Dead. (I didn't like the Dead as much as Rachel did, but I enjoyed the culture surrounding the band.) Through my mom's manager, we were able to get tickets from the Dead's head of ticket sales. We ended up being pretty friendly with him, and backstage at one concert he introduced us to Weir. After we made our first demo, we played it for him at his house in Palo Alto, and he was supportive. I didn't know whether he actually liked our music—he was probably aghast—but he suggested we put a band together.

To find a drummer, bass player, guitarist, and keyboardist, we relied on word of mouth and recommendations. We were so inexperienced that we auditioned players in our apartment—in Amy's room, in fact. We still didn't have a drum set, but we'd at least moved up to a MIDI electronic drum machine, which we hooked up to external drum pads. We hired our drummer, Alan, without even hearing him play on a real drum kit.

Alan had been a lawyer but hadn't practiced law in years because he preferred doing music. He reminded me of the Scarecrow in *The Wizard of Oz*—rather thin, a bit nerdy, and really sweet. Dorothy had the closest relationship with the Scarecrow, just as we did with Alan. He was a mensch. He was totally into the band, and he and Rachel became like brother and sister, spending many hours together playing or listening to music. He lived only a block away, and since he was single he spent most of his time hanging out with us.

Next we hired a bass player, Simon, and a keyboardist, Tommy. Tommy was our joker—a short, stocky guy with a straight-laced haircut. He was always in a good mood, always cutting up. I thought of him as the Lion in *The Wizard of Oz*, because he was the comic relief, just like Bert Lahr had been in the movie.

Simon didn't seem part of *Oz* at all. He was the only married guy in the band, and quite eccentric. He had longish, dirty-blond hair and an angular physique, over which he liked to drape odd costumes. One day he'd dress as a Hasidic Jew, for example, and another day in a safari outfit. We never got to know Simon that well, as the being in the band was more of a job to him. For the rest of us, it was our lives.

After hiring these three, we still needed a guitarist, but we auditioned tons of musicians without success. This was the late 1980s, the time of "hair" bands, so guys would come in with pink guitars and hair two feet high and try to infuse Def Leppard solos inappropriately into our songs. We finally auditioned someone we liked, but he was an older studio musician who didn't want to play in a band for free. We had very little money (we supported ourselves by working occasional telemarketing jobs that Amy hooked us up with), but we wanted to make a better demo, so we hired this guy to play guitar on it and decided to look for a permanent guitarist after we got a record deal.

We rehearsed in Amy's tiny room, with Alan in one corner playing the electronic drum kit, Tommy playing a keyboard sampler in the middle of the room, Simon standing somewhere, the guitarist sitting on Amy's single bed, and Rachel and I finding whatever we could to sit on. Most of these guys probably thought we were insane, but we had this totally naive enthusiasm. We never even considered renting a rehearsal space. Why should we, we thought, when we had Amy's bed to play on?

By summer 1989, we were ready to record our second demo. Around that time, Joan and Scotti came to New York for a visit. When Rachel and I would go to L.A., we'd usually stay at Scotti's, who now lived next door to Joan. (Scotti had bought the house in case she needed to care for her husband, and when he died suddenly she moved in.) At this point Scotti didn't have much of a social life—she'd sit in front of the TV all day, drinking coffee and smoking while watching sports and the stock ticker—so we weren't putting her out. When Joan and Scotti came to New York, they'd be sure to see us as well.

On this trip, Rachel and I decided to take Joan and Scotti to dinner at our favorite French restaurant in the

West Village, Chez Ma Tante. Joan showed up all in white, which we thought was the funniest thing in the world—such a tourist! She was also wearing a lot of expensive jewelry. She might as well have written "mug me" across her forehead. Joan dressed adventurously and glamorously and usually looked great—she never, ever looked grungy, even in a T-shirt and jeans—but she occasionally miscalculated.

After dinner we went to one of our favorite lesbian bars in the Village, a dive called the Cubby Hole, and met up with some friends. We were just hanging out, having a good time, and at some point I found myself away from the group, standing with Joan.

"So, are you about to become a rock star?" she asked me.

Immediately I got embarrassed and looked down at my shoes, just as I had when I was thirteen.

"Not yet," I said modestly, "but things are going pretty well. We've just started working on a demo with the new band. These guys are great musicians and really nice. We hang out with them a lot."

"That's great, Chas. I've always liked the songs you've written, and I love your voice." Joan had heard me sing at the Strasberg Institute, where I wrote and performed a song for an original play we put on, and she'd also heard me sing with my dad in Palm Springs. I'd also played her some of the songs I'd written in high school. At least I had *one* fan.

"Thanks," I said, still feeling shy. "How's everything with you?"

I was expecting some simple, polite answer, but suddenly, in a dramatic move, Joan almost collapsed into me, crying. Over the loud music, she yelled in my ear, "I have cancer."

I hoped I'd heard her wrong, even though I knew I hadn't. I was stunned. This news compounded an already bad day, during which I'd learned that my friend Michael, a dancer in my mom's Vegas show whom I'd had a big crush on when I was twelve, had died of AIDS. I'd only learned a month earlier that he was sick, and his longtime boyfriend had told me Michael wouldn't be around much longer. I'd been planning to come to Los Angeles to see him, then got the news that it was too late. Now this.

"I'm sorry," was all I could feebly say, and I held her while she cried on my shoulder. I didn't know what else to do.

Once Joan regained her composure, I found Rachel to tell her what was going on and that we had to leave the bar. We went back to our apartment, where Joan told us more about her illness. She had found a lump under her right arm, she said, and when she went to the doctor they found two other lumps—one in her throat and one in her groin area. A biopsy showed she had non-Hodgkin's lymphoma, a cancer of the lymph nodes. There's no cure for the disease, the doctors said, but they told her that the type she had was easily treatable with radiation and mild doses of oral chemotherapy. They also warned her that the lymphoma could change at some point and become more aggressive.

"The doctor first said that the life expectancy is five years with this kind of cancer," said Joan, who was just forty-three at the time. "But then he said that was just the minimum and that I could live five, ten, fifteen years, or more."

When we asked how she was handling all this, she said she was really blown away, unable to figure it out. She had always been a healthy person who ate well, exercised regularly, and didn't smoke. She was confused and scared and having trouble getting her mind around the idea that she had an incurable disease.

I was having just as hard a time coming to terms with it. Joan had always seemed immortal to me and had been such a large part of my life for so many years. When you're young, you take physical health for granted—your own and that of those around you. Joan certainly didn't look sick; she looked as beautiful as ever. I couldn't fully comprehend the news, so I latched onto every positive thing she mentioned, especially that this sort of cancer was treatable with radiation and could be put into remission. As for the prognosis of her living five more years, that seemed like a fairly long time to me. I was only twenty years old: Five years was a quarter of my life.

Shortly after that startling evening, Joan flew back to Los Angeles, where she began radiation treatments. She ended up getting a horrible sore throat from the radiation to her neck, but otherwise the treatment went well and did indeed put her into remission. The only lasting effect, she said, was that she never again had to shave her right armpit.

*

Over the next months I didn't have much time to think about Joan, as our band was busy working on our second demo. Since we couldn't afford studio time, we made do with the recording equipment at our apartment and at Alan's, where he had a fairly sophisticated digital setup. We programmed all the drums, recorded the piano tracks on a high-end sampler, and for the vocals we rented expensive tube microphones and hired an engineer recommended by a friend of ours. We even rented some baffles to improve the sound and made a windscreen for the mike out of a coat hanger and panty hose—which worked quite well.

We recorded three tracks, which took several months to complete. Once they were done we had to mix them, and for that we needed a studio. So we rented one and mixed for twenty-four straight hours, downing coffee like it was water. Generally people take a day or two to mix *one* song; doing three in one day is crazy, because you get pretty punchy and your ears don't work very well. Everything starts to sound the same.

After we finally finished we went home and rested our ears a bit, then listened to the mix again. It sounded terrible: muddy and awful. None of us had ever mixed a record before (including our engineer), and we suddenly realized why there are professionals who do nothing but mix records. We were tremendously depressed, since it had cost us $1,000 for those twenty-four hours and we didn't have another grand to redo the mix. Even if we could have come up with the money, we didn't feel confident we could do a better job the second time around. It hit us hard that we didn't know what we were doing.

But we were about to get lucky. Out of the blue, I received an unrelated phone call from Bill "Bumper" Sammeth, who'd been my mom's manager since I was a kid and who happened to be in town. He had worked for many years with well-known manager Sandy Gallin, and he'd handled such entertainers as Dolly Parton, Joan Rivers, Olivia Newton-John, the Osmonds, and KC and the Sunshine Band. Since I had Bumper on the phone, I told him what had just happened and how we felt our tracks were really good despite the bad mix. I asked him to come over to listen and give us some advice. He did, and agreed that while the mix was terrible, the tracks were pretty good. When he returned to Los Angeles, he obtained some free studio time for us to do another mix. He also called in favors from producer Rich Matthews and engineer Sam Fox (who had worked on some of my mom's records), and they agreed to give us a free day of mixing.

So Rachel and I and a couple of our bandmates flew to Los Angeles, where we spent an amazing day. Everyone in the studio was so professional, and they made our tracks sound as professional as possible. We instantly fell in love with Rich, who was very charming and taught us an extraordinary amount in only a day.

Bumper then did us another favor by arranging a meeting for us with John Kalodner, the main artists and repertoire person at Geffen Records, my mom's label. Kalodner—an eccentric-looking guy with long dark hair, a long beard like the guys in ZZ Top have, and John Lennon-type glasses who wore white suits and sounded like Bert on *Sesame Street*—was the most successful, well-known A&R guy in the record business. I'm sure it didn't hurt that both Bumper and Kalodner were connected with my mom, but I don't think Bumper would have even made the call if he didn't think we had something to offer. He asked Kalodner something like "Can you listen to these kids' demo and give them some advice?"

Rachel and I met with Kalodner at Geffen Records and played him our demo—and he reacted very positively. He asked whether we'd taken it to any other record company, and we said no. Actually, Geffen was the last place we considered bringing it to, since we wanted to keep our career separate from my mom's. But when John Kalodner tells you he thinks you have a home at Geffen Records, it's pretty hard to say, "Yeah, but my mom's on your label..."

"I love you guys," he told Rachel and me. "I love the voices, I love the songs, I like your look—but I want to check out this band of yours." Obviously, he wasn't overly impressed by anyone's musical talents on the demo, and more importantly he wanted to see what our band looked like and how old the players were. As I said, this was the era of blow-dried hair bands, and image was everything. Rachel and I got a little paranoid hearing his concerns, since we knew that none of our guys was ready for MTV—none had long hair, for starters. Alan had longish hair but was starting to lose it; Tommy's hair was just an inch longer than a crewcut; and Simon had recently shaved off his long hair after he'd gotten oil in it during a motorcycle accident. Age-wise, our band members were all in their thirties, and Simon was married. We were hardly the hip young hair band we knew Kalodner was looking for.

But when we left the Geffen Records offices and met up with our bandmates outside, we didn't talk to them about their hair. Instead we told them the good news, and soon we were all hugging and jumping up and down on Sunset Boulevard like idiots.

Kalodner wanted us to go back to New York and spend a few weeks preparing a live showcase so he could see our band perform and hear more of our material. We were thrilled but panicked—we'd never played live before. We'd never even played outside the apartment, so the concept of *standing* while playing would be a leap forward. We also didn't have many songs on our play list, and the best of our repertoire was on the demo. We had our work cut out for us.

It was around Thanksgiving, and Kalodner wanted to see us again at the beginning of January, so we had about a month to prepare for the showcase. When we returned to New York, we started to rehearse—in a studio, finally—and auditioned guitarists like crazy. We finally found a guy named Mitch whom we liked a lot, and he completed our unnamed band. Mitch was the best-looking guy in the group, although he wore his hair in an unfortunate mullet when we first met him. He was half-Jewish, half-Japanese, and thus rather exotic looking, with dark hair and dark eyes. Mitch was also the most rock 'n' roll of the guys, both musically and in the sense that he drank a lot of beer and hard alcohol while the rest of us were pretty straight-laced at the time. His drinking didn't affect his work habits, though, and he turned out to be quite dedicated to the band. I thought of him as the Tin Man in *Oz*. He was a sweet guy, but a little reserved in his metallic armor.

Our band was complete, but we still needed to develop a stronger visual identity. Kalodner's remarks worried us, since we knew our lack of a "look" could cause problems down the road.

✳

In the midst of all the stress of rehearsing for our showcase and developing a rapport with the band, my life turned completely upside down for a completely different reason: During the week of Christmas, the tabloid *The Star* outed me. "Cher Shattered When Daughter Says 'I'm Gay' " read the ridiculous headline.

What they printed was a story about my mom finally learning that I was gay two years before. There wasn't a lot of information in it, and they didn't have a picture of Rachel and me together, but all the tabloids need is a kernel of fact that they can blow up like popcorn. The way I found out about the whole mess was that my mom's publicist, Lois Smith of PMK, had been sent an advanced copy of the article, probably to see if I wanted to comment on it. She was freaked out when she called to tell me, and I panicked too. All I wanted to know was, "Can we stop it before it's printed?" Much to my dismay, she said "No." Since it was true, nothing could be done.

The outing didn't stop with that one article. Follow-up stories talked about me being in a band with my girlfriend, though Rachel's name was never mentioned. Some of the articles were surprisingly accurate about our daily life, saying that I cooked a lot and that we went bowling. Others were ludicrously inaccurate, like the one saying I shot porno films while attending NYU. We knew someone close to us must have been talking to the tabloids, but we never discovered who it was. And we couldn't sue over the lies, because then the truth about me being gay would have to come out as well.

I was unnerved by this sudden onslaught, afraid it would wreck our potential deal with Geffen Records. The outing also disrupted my rather carefree relationship with Rachel. Once we'd decided to go into music, we didn't go to gay bars as often, but we hadn't stopped completely. If people knew who I was at a bar, they didn't make a big deal about it. Our band had even gone to Gay Pride the previous year. Now all our open behavior would have to stop, and we were slammed back into the darkest corner of the closet. In the coming weeks, Lois Smith even set me up on dates with men, which made the gay press criticize me for *not* coming out. I couldn't win.

Someone told me that as long as no one came up with a picture of Rachel and me together, we could deny everything. We became so paranoid that someone would break into our house and steal photos that we took every picture we had of us together and stored them at Rachel's parents' house on Long Island. Then we still went crazy thinking someone might have snapped a picture of us at a party. Rumor had it that the tabloids would pay $10,000 for such a photo. *The Star* did run a picture of us walking down the street in New York with another woman, but we weren't even touching each other. Rachel and I joked that we should have just taken a picture of ourselves on the street and collected the $10,000. Lord knows we could have used it.

Reporters started to call us and leave notes at our apartment. They even harassed Rachel's family, trying to get them to talk. Rachel and I left from different exits whenever we went out, and we no longer went out alone together. We made sure we always had men around us, because that's what my mom advised us to do.

Every Sunday I felt a mounting dread, since the tabloids would hit the stands the next day. On Monday mornings, without fail, some friend would call and say, "Did you see this one?" One time Rachel's ex, Donna, who was a close friend of ours, called us on a Monday morning, and before she had a chance to say anything I asked her in a panic, "What is it?! What did you see?!"

"Nothing," she said, sounding confused. "I was just calling to say hi."

"Don't ever call me on a Monday morning!" I barked.

Fortunately, Geffen Records remained cool about the whole thing and were still interested in us. As promised, John Kalodner flew out to New York for our showcase, bringing with him a female A&R person, Mary Gormley, who worked out of Geffen's New York office. We ended up liking her a lot.

But our performance wasn't that great, and Kalodner wasn't thrilled with our bandmates. He did like Rachel and me, he told us, despite how green we were on stage. So he said he'd give us a six-month development deal, during which time he'd hook us up with a stylist and arrange for us to do gigs around New York. It was a good deal, providing us money for rehearsal space and clothes. And it gave us some time to get our feet wet and see if we could end up on the same page as Kalodner in terms of whether we'd keep the band we had.

"Either you'll come around to my way of thinking, I'll come around to yours, or we'll part company," he told us. That seemed fair. It didn't even occur to us that we could turn down Geffen Records and seek out a different label. We'd hitched ourselves to them, and soon we were off on quite a ride.

✳

During the six-month development period, we wanted more than anything to prove ourselves as a band. Except for Simon, our bandmates had become our best friends—we'd rehearse with them, go out to dinner with them, and then play poker all night with them. We were especially close with Alan; hardly a day went by that we didn't see him.

A wonderful group of other friends surrounded us too, hanging out at our rehearsals and coming to every gig. They were like our very own Deadheads. People dropped by our apartment all the time, where I cooked a lot. (I'd inherited the Italian cooking gene from my dad, and the Balducci's and Gristede's grocery accounts from my mom.) Even with the press butting into my private life, I was still having a great time in New York, filled with music and people I loved.

We liked to party, and occasionally we indulged in "whippets"—nitrous oxide cartridges used to produce whipped cream. We bought them by the box at head shops and inserted them into empty whipped cream canisters, then sprayed and inhaled, which gave us a stratospheric rush for about thirty seconds. Even so, we were hardly crazed druggies: We were just making a feeble attempt at the rock 'n' roll lifestyle. None of us were into hard drugs like cocaine. At the time, I believed I didn't have an addictive bone in my body, because I could take or leave alcohol and drugs. I was even scared of taking pain medication. Once when I had a painfully infected wisdom tooth, I wouldn't even take the Tylenol with codeine I was prescribed.

None of us was a wild thing—we just liked to get drunk or do whippets. We weren't trying to escape reality either, because except for the tabloids, reality was a blast. We were just partying because we were in our twenties, when life is all about having fun.

To improve our image, we started working with a stylist named Leeza, who we liked a lot. Our poor bandmates, though—we were putting them through hell to get their look right. Some of them got hair extensions, Simon wore a wig, and Alan even got a hair transplant. We wanted so desperately for them to stay in the band.

In retrospect, the clothes we ended up wearing were obnoxious—brightly colored '6os throwbacks. Leeza created her own signature items, such as a pair of blue jeans with old couch upholstery sewn on or hand-painted black Beatles boots. Certain items were cool, but she put everything together in a way that purposefully clashed.

Besides changing clothes and hairstyles, we kept changing our band's name every time we played, partly to throw the press off our trail and partly because we hadn't made a firm decision yet. For one gig we were called Vicious Rumors (I wonder why!) and another time The Bandwagon. Our wildest name was Herman and the Skrankdogs. "Skrank" was the word we used when we had a weak hand in poker ("This hand is skrank"), and Herman was the nickname Mitch gave almost everyone. Later, Rachel and I even named our dog Herman.

About two months after our first performance for him, John Kalodner flew to New York to see us play at the Cat Club, a small downtown rock music venue that held several hundred people sitting at tables. At that time, my mom was dating a really great guy, guitarist Richie Sambora from Bon Jovi, and he came to the gig on his own. (I was too nervous to ask my mom to come see us.) We ended up going out afterward with Richie and his lawyer—who later became our lawyer—and spent the night partying at different bars around town, finally ending up at an all-night diner.

Our performance went pretty well, and John seemed

happy with the progress we'd made. But there was some unpleasant backlash from the gig: The publicist for Geffen Records had kicked a photographer out of the club and had taken his roll of film, so the photographer got pissed off and sold a completely false story to the tabloids. He claimed that everything we had was my mom's—our band equipment, our lawyer, even a tour bus that belonged to another band on the bill. He also wrote that Rachel and I sang "I Got You, Babe" together while looking starrily into each other's eyes. We were getting a bad taste of what the press could be like, and it was upsetting.

We had another unsavory run-in with the press during a gig upstate in Woodstock, where we opened for another Geffen Records band. We were having a great time there, staying in a cabin with our friends. Before the show, a rock critic from a New York–area newspaper came to interview us; it was the first press we'd done as a band. He spent time with us during our sound check, interviewed each band member separately, then watched our show. I don't know what I did to offend this critic, other than tell him I wasn't exactly sure how to spell our drummer's last name. I'm a notoriously bad speller, and I was nervous and shy during the interview.

We ended up playing a good gig, and the guy seemed to like us, but while he raved about our band and our material in his review—even suggesting that one of our songs would be a hit single—he continually knocked *me* for having a so-called attitude. "And she doesn't even know how to spell her band members' names," he wrote. I didn't understand why he felt it necessary to cut me down on a personal level.

After the Woodstock gig, Geffen put Rachel and me

together with various songwriters to try to come up with additional material. Our experiences ranged from the wonderfully creative to the absurd, and only one of the songs we cowrote (with singer-songwriter Martin Briley) during that time, "2 of 1," made it to our record. Even though the songs we worked on didn't get recorded, we enjoyed writing with Richie Sambora, with whom we had developed a relationship. We also learned a lot working with Desmond Child, who cowrote hits for groups like Aerosmith and my mom and later cowrote Ricky Martin's "Livin' La Vida Loca." We didn't actually write a song with Desmond, but he taught me a lot about lyric structure. Rachel had been writing most of our lyrics, which were esoteric and poetic but rather incomprehensible (she was a Deadhead, after all.) Desmond pointed out that lyrics have to have meaning—which seems obvious, but I guess it wasn't to us. After that experience with him, I began writing lyrics as well as music for our songs.

By the end of the summer of 1990, John Kalodner wanted to hear a rehearsal tape of our new songs to see what direction we were going in. We had some pretty good new songs, but we had absolutely no idea how to arrange anything. Despite our fondness for most of our bandmates, we started to realize the band's shortcomings. I had no musical training, and Rachel had very little, so we hoped the other players would help us arrange what we'd written, but they couldn't. We were starting to see that they probably couldn't help us fully realize the potential of our music.

To make the rehearsal tape, we brought in Sam Fox from L.A., the guy who had mixed our demo, and he worked with us for a week. We sent a recording of that session to John Kalodner, and although he liked a couple of the songs, he hated the arrangements. We were really panicking now, since our development deal was about up. We were supposed to do another demo, but things weren't sounding right. We were discouraged, to say the least.

So we decided to call Rich Matthews, the producer who had seemed to understand our music so well while we were remixing our second demo. We felt he was the only one who could help us, so we asked him to produce our third demo, in Los Angeles, at Sam Fox's home studio.

Rich was in his early forties, moderately handsome, with a beard and a small bald spot. He was quite a stylish guy, one of the few straight men I've known who was daring with his clothes, always experimenting with different hats, scarves, vests, and strong colors (purple was a particular favorite). He was also unbelievably funny and charming, and one of the most talented people I'd ever met.

Geffen Records liked that we were working with him, but they still didn't like our band. We'd been having doubts too, but when they eventually asked us to kick out some of our players it was painful. Not only were they our bandmates, but some of them were our best friends. It wasn't that hard for us to fire Simon, since he was weird and no one particularly liked him, but then we were asked to fire Tommy because of his looks, and that was really heartbreaking. He was a great guy, and we cared a lot about him. Rachel and I remained hopeful, though, that if we sacrificed Simon and Tommy—whom we replaced with other friends of Alan's—we'd be able to keep Alan and Mitch.

We flew to Los Angeles to make the demo without any of our band members, because Rich wanted to use his own guys. Since this was the demo that would decide our fate with Geffen, we didn't want to take any chances, so we immediately agreed to that. We were quickly bonding with Rich on a creative level; we loved what he was doing with our music. We were also constantly siding with him against Sam, who challenged Rich nonstop in the studio. Sam was a very good engineer but wanted coproduction credit on the album. We liked Rich's musical choices better, but it was a sticky situation, because Sam was letting us use his studio for free and we couldn't risk alienating him.

We ended up recording three songs in two weeks of work, and the demo sounded amazing. We worked with great musicians who played much better than our own guys. The demo achieved the sound Rachel and I had always hoped for but weren't sophisticated enough to create on our own.

During the recording sessions, however, things went from bad to worse between Rich and Sam. Right before we turned the demo in to John Kalodner, Sam made the foolish mistake of calling John and saying the recording wasn't his vision and that he'd been constantly overruled by Rich, Rachel, and me. John, however, loved the demo and immediately offered us a recording deal. That effectively ended Sam's involvement with us; he had slit his own throat.

The contract offer from Geffen also ended our relationship with our band, since Rachel and I realized they weren't as proficient players as the studio guys. In hindsight, if we hadn't felt such an urgency about signing with

Geffen Records we could all have taken the time to develop individually as musicians and collectively as a band. Since we'd been offered a record deal, though, we knew we couldn't spend the next two years playing dives and hoping to develop our chops. I think most people, if given the chance to sign with Geffen Records, would have done what we did and said yes.

As our music took a huge leap forward, we had to leave the camaraderie of our homegrown musical community and enter the clutches of the record business. That was the trade-off we were making, and to be honest, we'd never again have as much fun making music as we had in our New York days. We'd been like a tribe, a grunge band before grunge became popular. It's ironic: Part of the reason our career never took off is that the whole Seattle grunge sound—which mixed the independent spirit of punk music with a distorted, metal-music guitar sound—became hot just as our non-grunge-sounding record was finally released. If the record company hadn't made us fire our band, we might have recorded the sort of album that would have been more along the lines of what ended up being popular from groups such as Soundgarden, Nirvana, and Pearl Jam.

*

Since Geffen Records is located in Los Angeles, where Rich lived, Rachel, Amy, and I decided to move there too, renting a two-bedroom house in Sherman Oaks. We started writing new songs with Rich, scrapping all but two of the compositions we'd been working on.

Each time we came up with a batch of five new songs, we went to the Geffen offices and played them acoustically for John Kalodner. After we wrote about twenty good songs, we planned to demo them on Rich's four-track equipment. Actually, those demos would turn out better than the record we'd eventually make. They had a cool edge, and they weren't overproduced. Of course, we didn't know then that we should have kept everything simple.

Rachel and I were improving as songwriters—we were more focused now—but we still didn't have all that much to write about. Mainly we wrote about being happy in love, being frustrated by love, or, at our most edgy, being pawns of the record industry. The one experience about which we would have had the most interesting things to say was our tabloid outing—but we were still way too deep in the closet to sing about it.

One of the things the record company insisted we do was record a song by Diane Warren for our record. She's one of the most successful pop songwriters (she's written big hits for people like Céline Dion, Toni Braxton, and many others), but her songs weren't exactly our style. But Geffen basically gave us an ultimatum: "You either record this song or you don't make the record." So we caved and recorded Warren's "Breathless." It didn't feel like us at all.

On top of the pressure coming from the record company, Rich was turning out not to be as perfect as we'd imagined. He was starting to flirt with Rachel, even though he was married and knew Rachel and I were a couple. That didn't stop him, however, from making subtle innuendos to Rachel every time I'd leave the room. I found his behavior annoying and disappointing, but I wasn't particularly jealous because I knew Rachel wasn't interested.

It was confusing. Rich had the kind of energy that made him seem as if he were being enthusiastic about the music when he was being flirtatious, so it was sometimes hard to tell where he was coming from. Rachel and I felt strangely powerless in the situation. We figured we'd been signed by Geffen because of Rich and the demo we'd made with him, and we weren't confident we could do such high-caliber work without him. He knew he had us over a barrel, at least psychologically, so he could lord that over us. There was nothing we could do to change his behavior except fire him, and we certainly couldn't do that.

*

As the pressure of our budding recording career heated up, at least I could turn to Joan for relief. Fortunately, the cancer hadn't affected her life too greatly. About a year after her initial radiation treatments, she went on oral chemotherapy, which had few side effects other than making her feel tired. When I started spending time with Joan in Los Angeles, I didn't think about her illness at all.

We weren't flirting, though Joan was such a warm and touchy person that our affectionate behavior might have made it seem as if we were. Almost all of my friends, except Rachel, developed a crush on Joan at one time or another. She was just the kind of person who exuded sexuality, plus she really listened, seemed genuinely interested in what you were saying, and was very attractive in a feminine way. People were completely drawn to her, and she didn't mind the attention a bit.

Even though I grew up in Los Angeles, I didn't have that many friends in town, so Rachel and I often hung out with Joan and her crowd. Joan was an entertainer extraordinaire, so hospitable and welcoming. We called her house on Kling Street in Studio City the "Hooky House," since it was a great place to go and escape any sort of responsibility. Your problems didn't seem to exist when you went there. The house itself—a single-story, flat-roofed structure from the 1960s that had huge front and back yards shaded with trees—wasn't extravagant but had a well-furnished, conservative, homey appearance. Since Joan didn't have to work, she seemed to be permanently playing hooky, though she kept herself busy by working out, shopping, and social-izing. She acted just like the wife of a rich husband—except she didn't have a husband.

The Hooky House was the site of many notorious par-ties, attended mostly by gay women and a smattering of gay men. We sometimes had a lot to drink and got pretty silly, but if we got too silly we spent the night there so we wouldn't have to drive home. At one point it became quite the tradition to drink tequila at Joan's parties, and shots of tequila became my drink of choice. Tequila has an almost drug-like effect—it's a very "up" drink, and when you drink really good tequila, you can drink even more than usual because it doesn't burn so much going down.

But we also spent more dignified time at Joan's. I especially liked her longtime girlfriend Leslie, whom I'd known since I was a kid. She was a bit insecure and a real drama queen, but she was fun to be around. Rachel and I sometimes spent entire weekends with Joan and Les, coming over to the Hooky House on a Friday night and not leaving until Monday morning. We'd eat dinner together, go to movies, play board games, and go shopping. Joan and Leslie were our only friends who were a lesbian couple, and even though they were considerably older than us, they were a lot of fun to be with.

It's not surprising, then, that Joan and Leslie were the first people we talked to about the situation with Rich after it began to escalate. It came up while we were hanging out on a weekend afternoon in Joan's living room. Joan was getting something from the kitchen, Leslie was in the bathroom, and Rachel and I were on Joan's big L-shaped off-white couch, talking intensely. We were clearly unnerved, and Joan could sense it as she walked in. We lowered our voices.

"You guys OK? Do you need to be alone?" Joan asked us.

"We're fine," I said. "We're just having some problems with Rich."

"I thought you guys loved working with him. The demo sounds so great."

"It's not about the music," Rachel said. "It's a more personal thing."

Les walked in from the bathroom and quickly realized we were discussing something serious. "What's up?" she asked us.

"I don't know, but I think I'm about to find out," said Joan. "They're having some kind of problem with Rich."

Leslie plopped down on the couch next to Joan. She loved poking her nose into things. "I thought everything was going so well with him."

"The music is going fine," I reiterated.

"The problem is the way he's treating *me*," Rachel blurted.

"I thought he was like a musical mentor to you," said Leslie.

There was a pause as Joan and Leslie looked at her, waiting for her to speak. Rachel took a long breath, then finally said, "He's been coming on to me."

The mood in the room suddenly shifted. Joan and Leslie had expected something far less serious. It wasn't something as simple as Rich showing up late for meetings or not returning our phone calls.

"What?!" they exclaimed in unison.

Rachel sighed, ready to finally unload her burden on someone besides me. "It started on Christmas, when Chas was away in Aspen," she said. "He called me up, and we started talking about our work schedule and about this new song we were working on, and then he made some sexually suggestive comments."

"Like what?" Leslie asked.

"I don't want to go into detail—it's really embarrassing. Let's just say he wasn't subtle or just flirtatious. He was completely out of line. Since then, every time we're alone together in the studio, he starts in on me. The gist of it is that he wants me, we're soul mates, and he feels like he might be falling in love with me."

"I thought he knew about you and Chas," Leslie said.

"He does, but it doesn't seem to make any difference to him ," Rachel said.

"How do you respond to him when he talks like that to you?" asked Joan, looking concerned.

"I don't know how to respond. I guess I try to defuse it by laughing, or trying to get him back to what we're working on. But nothing—even telling him flat-out that I'm in love with Chas—seems to stop him."

Joan turned to me. "How are *you* handling all this?"

"He's never done it to me, and he doesn't do it when I'm in the room," I explained.

Joan put a hand on my shoulder. "That's not what I mean. How are you dealing with the fact he keeps coming on to your girlfriend?"

"It makes me furious," I told her, "but I feel like there's nothing I can do. We need him for our music."

Leslie and Joan looked dumbfounded and turned to Rachel, hoping she'd say something that made more sense. When she remained silent, Joan said, "You can get *anyone* to produce your music. There are a million producers in this town."

"Rachel, I can't believe that you of all people would put up with this," Leslie chimed in.

Rachel, a tough feminist, seemed to be the last person to take this kind of abuse. In fact, after we saw the film *The Accused*, in which Jodie Foster's character gets gang-raped, Rachel called our male friends to rant and rave about how all men were capable of rape. For a while she even stopped talking to a dear male friend of hers when he expressed doubts about abortion rights. Rachel didn't take shit from anybody and wasn't afraid to speak her mind.

"I know, believe me," she said. "But we need him."

"I still don't understand. Why do you think you need him so much that you'll put up with anything?" Joan asked Rachel.

"We'd never have gotten signed if it wasn't for him. He created our whole sound."

"You mean to tell me that if Rich Matthews died tomorrow your music career would be over?" Joan asked.

Rachel and I silently mulled that one over. Then we both answered, "Yeah."

Joan and Leslie looked at us like we were crazy.

✴

Over the next few months we got together with Rich about four times a week to write songs. Nothing much had changed in Rich's behavior toward Rachel—he kept coming on to her, and we kept trying to grin and bear it as best we could. But the situation was affecting my relationship with Rachel. She was acting like an abused woman, afraid to tell me some of the things he said to her. We got into fights over completely insignificant things, and I'd find out later that she had felt ashamed about some situation with Rich and had lashed out at me instead. I felt terrible because, as her girlfriend, I wasn't doing anything to help remedy the problem.

Rich was showing the Mr. Hyde side of his personality: If Rachel didn't respond the way he wanted her to, he went on strike. When he wasn't being charming, he could be a mean, nasty, hit-below-the-belt kind of guy who was great at homing in on someone's weaknesses and fears. He tried to make us doubt everyone—except him, of course. Meanwhile, God only knows what he was telling people behind our backs; he was a master of the divide-and-conquer strategy.

I wish I could blame all of the problems between Rachel and me on Rich, but our relationship had cooled for reasons having nothing to do with him. By this time we'd been together three years and the passion had waned. We'd been great together, totally in love, but as our music career took off, the *career* became sexy to us, not each other. We stopped nurturing our relationship, and it gradually became more of a work partnership.

I don't think either of us realized what was happening, though I often talked to Joan about how my sex life had dwindled and she gave me advice on how to rekindle the romance. But since everything between Rachel and me remained so focused on making music, I didn't get much of a chance to put Joan's advice into action. I had grown up with Rachel, and we were still incredibly close, but our relationship and our career had fused. There wasn't much room in between for us to be lovers.

As for the music, Rachel was much more driven than I was. She lived for our album. She was tireless in the studio, never wanting to leave, while I got bored more easily. She was sacrificing everything for this career, because she truly loved doing it. Back on that bridge in Paris, I sensed how much she loved music, and that's why I had asked her to be my partner. I needed her drive. To me, music was a logical career step to take when I had no idea what I wanted to do. I never had that deep love of music that Rachel did. I figured her passion would be enough to carry us both along. But her all-stops-out commitment to our career also put her in a more authoritative position over me when it came to making our record. That caused problems too, because I resented always being told what to do and how to do it.

The good news was that despite our personal and professional problems, the music we were writing was coming out great. We played tapes for our friends and they were blown away. They even began to understand why we were sticking with Rich, despite our complaints (which everyone had heard by now). If Rachel had said to me at any time that she couldn't take his behavior any more, I would have said, "Fine." But she didn't. At some point we even spoke to the record company about it and they said, "So fire him."

"We don't want to," we told them.

"Well, there's nothing else we can do about it."

I might not have realized how much my feelings for Rachel had changed if I hadn't begun to feel so strongly about Joan.

On Cinco de Mayo, 1991, Joan planned an outing with a bunch of friends. We all loved Cinco de Mayo because, among other reasons, it gave us yet another excuse to drink fine tequila. But Rachel and I were on a strict deadline to get the lyrics for our songs completed, so we had to stay in and work that night.

When we finished at about eleven P.M., the doorbell rang. We opened the door to find Joan and Scotti, Hugh and Kim (a gay male couple who lived down the street from us), and Faye, a woman Joan had dated a few times. Scotti was really drunk; I'd never seen her so smashed. Remember, Scotti was much older than us—she was my grandmother's age. Maybe she'd have a beer at a party, but I'd never seen her really let her hair down. Instead, she was usually just a grumbly old dyke in a flannel shirt who gave us "kids" disapproving looks and told us to keep it down when we were too noisy. She had long ago stopped having lovers because she'd had her heart broken so often by straight women. The biggest event in her life had become playing bingo twice a week with a bunch of other older women. She usually won too. Scotti definitely had that "unlucky in love, lucky at cards" thing going for her.

We were in hysterics seeing Scotti so plastered and whooping it up. She wasn't editing what she was saying, and she had some very definite opinions about Joan's choice of girlfriends. Leslie drove her insane, because she was always making a scene or picking a fight with Joan, and Connie was an idiot, Scotti thought. She found Faye, however, to be sweet and uncomplicated—but unattractive. And that's just what she wanted to tell us that night.

"That Faye," she slurred, "she's sure nothing to look at, but boy is she nice!" Of course, Faye was well within earshot of this declaration, but perhaps she was too drunk herself to comprehend the backhanded compliment.

Rachel and I watched with amusement as our friends stumbled around the house. Everyone was hungry, so Joan and I—the two cooks of the bunch—got marching orders to whip up something to eat. Soon we were alone in the kitchen, as everyone else had gone into the living room to continue drinking and listen to music.

Joan and I decided to cook a batch of quesadillas, and when they were done we called out, "Come and get it!"

Rachel and Kim eagerly walked into the kitchen. "Thank God. We're starving out here," Kim said.

"I didn't realize everyone was so hungry," Joan said. "Maybe we need to start another batch."

"In a minute," I told her. "I just want to go out back and have a cigarette." I asked Joan if she wanted to keep me company even though she didn't smoke—cigarettes, at least. She said yes, so we walked through the back bedroom and out the sliding glass door to the grassy yard. On the concrete walkway, we sat down side-by-side on a couple of lawn chairs.

"What's the deal with you and Faye?" I asked her. "Is it serious?" Actually, I was shocked that Joan was dating her, as she usually picked much more attractive and stylish women. Joan was so classy in comparison that it seemed like a mismatch.

"It's not serious at all," Joan said. "I just think she's a really nice person, and I enjoy spending time with her. I have a feeling we'll be just friends in the very near future." (Which turned out to be true.)

"Does Les know about her?"

"She knows there's someone else, because she cruised by the driveway the other day and saw an unfamiliar car. She's worried about having even more competition."

"Why don't you just settle down with Les?" I asked her. "You spend most of your time with her anyway, and you're not in love with Connie."

"I really care for Les, but not enough to see her exclusively. I love her, but I'm not *in* love with her. Enough about me—how's everything with you and Rachel?"

"I don't know. I don't really think about it." I paused for a moment. "I guess things are OK. It's hard working together—sometimes it seems our whole relationship these days is about work."

We both fell silent and just sat there, gazing up at the stars. Then Joan took my hand in her long, slender fingers and held it softly. At first I assumed she was making a comforting gesture in response to what I'd divulged. But her touch sent an electric current through me. I wondered whether she was feeling the same, so I caressed her hand in a way that clearly wasn't just friendly. She imme-diately reciprocated.

My mind raced with a tumble of thoughts. In the instant she had taken my hand, everything changed. The old feelings, which I'd thought I had safely wrapped up and tucked away, instantly returned, stronger than ever. More than that, those feelings suddenly seemed exactly right. With the history Joan and I had together, it was more than just a simple attraction we were feeling. It was as if the planets had finally aligned for us after so many things had thrown them off course. Joan and I had long shared a special friendship, on a number of levels, but with this renewed spark something much more was being created—something we could no longer ignore.

We sat there for a few minutes, silently holding hands, and only released our grip after someone came out yelling, "Where are those quesadillas?"

That was the sum of our contact that night, and we went back to the party pretending nothing had happened. But I knew there wasn't a middle ground for Joan and me. Either we were just friends, happily involved in other rela-tionships, or we were overwhelmed by lust and love for each other. For the rest of the night I couldn't stop think-ing about her touching my hand, and it was the first thing I thought about when I woke up the next morning.

In fact, Joan woke me up, with a call inviting Rachel and me to hang out at Hugh and Kim's pool. Rachel didn't feel well enough to go, though—she'd had too much tequila the night before, and *any* amount of alco-hol gave her a crippling hangover, which she then used more alcohol to cure. Rachel had been sober when I met her, after having had a drinking problem at age nineteen when her parents kicked her out of the house for being gay. For a couple of years she felt really out of control but didn't think she was an alcoholic. Then she began drinking again when we started our band in New York, because she got tired of being the only sober one. But I wasn't worried that she was an alcoholic now; it seemed she was just allergic to the stuff.

I was pleased that Rachel didn't want to go that day, since I desperately wanted to see Joan again and find out if what I thought had happened the night before really had. Amy came with me instead. As we arrived at Hugh and Kim's, I felt a familiar sense of excitement about seeing Joan.

Joan was in the pool by herself talking to Kim, who was sitting at the edge dangling his feet in the water. Hugh was in the house, and Faye was sleeping on a lounge chair. Amy made herself comfortable in a poolside chair to read a book.

I took my shirt off—I was wearing my version of a swimsuit: men's board shorts and a bathing suit top—and jumped in with Joan. As I swam over to greet her, I could tell immediately that she and I were on the same page. We kissed and hugged, and she leaned into me as I rested against the side of the pool. My arms were around her, and she was rubbing them. Even as we talked to Kim, we continued touching each other in a surprisingly open show of affection. If the others noticed, including Faye, no one seemed to pay us any mind, so we felt uninhibited.

Later, though, as I stood in the Jacuzzi with my arms wrapped around Joan, Kim said, "What's going on over here?"

"Don't you know we have a past?" Joan answered with a sly smile, then briefly told him how we had kissed when I was eighteen. She wanted him to believe that we were being affectionate out of friendship and nothing more.

Amy, too, was noticing a different sort of vibe as she periodically peered at us over the top of her book. The night before, I had told her about Joan holding my hand, and what it was like. I knew she would be discrete and wouldn't tell Rachel. Her response had merely been, "Oh, that's just Joan. She's held my hand before too." But later that day, when Amy and I were alone by the pool and I whispered, "I told you something's going on with Joan and me," she didn't argue. "I think you're right," she said.

After that day, the newfound intensity between Joan and me had nowhere to go. We had to put everything on ice again as Rachel and I returned to work. I needed to keep my focus, and I didn't have the energy to deal with Rachel, Rich, *and* Joan. Over the next few months, Joan and I continued to see each other as friends, and we were affectionate in a way that wouldn't draw any unwanted attention. Besides, we were rarely alone, since Rachel or Leslie was always around.

Around the beginning of September, Rachel and I finally had demo'd twenty songs for John Kalodner. We'd been working on them since January, first writing them, then playing them on acoustic guitars for John in his office, then having Rich record them with a band.

We took the demos to John's office at Geffen and sat there while he played them.

"You've got it, you've got the material," he said when he finished listening. "Let's book the studio."

We were psyched. We'd worked long and hard for this, starting out very green but honing our craft until we were ready to begin recording. It was more than we could have imagined that evening on the Pont Neuf in Paris.

Getting the go-ahead to start recording released a lot of stress for me. Maybe that's why I started flirting with Joan again.

It was early October, and Scotti invited us over to watch the World Series. She and Rachel wanted to see the game, but Joan and I weren't particularly interested (I've never been into baseball), so the two of us went next door to her house. We were in her kitchen talking, and suddenly we were holding hands. It felt like Cinco de Mayo all over again—we were chatting casually, then a meaningful silence fell over us.

"I think we need to talk about this," I said, looking down at our interwoven fingers.

"Let's go in the living room." Joan led me to the couch and we sat close, facing each other.

"Something's been going on between us since Cinco de Mayo, when you held my hand," I started. "Did I read that wrong?"

"No, I've felt the same way," she said, looking directly at me and smiling. My stomach was flipping, and my heart was pounding as I stared into those blue eyes. I wanted to draw out the deliciousness of the moment.

"What *are* you feeling?" I asked.

"Ever since that night, I've looked at you differently. I think a lot about you, what it would be like to be with you."

"I'm glad I'm not the only one. I know I'm supposed to fight this, but I feel like I'm losing the battle." I moved forward to kiss her, but she stopped me.

"How far are you willing to take this?" Joan asked cautiously. "Because I'm willing to take it all the way."

"I can't do that." I paused. "I can't do that to Rachel."

"That's what I thought." Joan was making it clear, without words, that she didn't want to start something that night that I couldn't finish.

I was really afraid what might happen to my career if I broke up with Rachel. I wasn't nearly as worried about hurting Rachel personally, because I was sure we had both lost the passion. Rachel had even said something about wishing she could sleep with groupies when we went on the road, which made me feel terrible. In fact, hearing that was the final straw: It allowed me to emotionally separate from her and allow my feelings for Joan to develop.

I didn't think Joan had any concerns about us being together. I was of age now, and our feelings for each other were sincere and undeniable. There was nothing holding Joan back except me. She wasn't even concerned about what my mom might think. My mom and Joan had been dancing and shopping buddies, but they'd never had a very deep friendship. There was history, though, between Joan and Scotti and my mom, so they were always on my mom's party invitation list.

Joan and I didn't resolve anything that night, but it became harder and harder to conceal the feelings between us. They were even becoming apparent to Rachel and Leslie, who joked about it, but with a cutting edge. Neither of them left Joan and me alone together if they could help it, and I'm sure they talked about us behind our backs. Sometimes they were very direct.

"What's going on between you and Joan?" Rachel or Les would ask.

"Nothing! Nothing's going on—you guys are crazy," I'd furiously answer. "We just have a very close friendship. We've always been like this."

I felt bad about being dishonest, but because of our album I felt compelled to lie. I was consumed with my feelings for Joan, and I desperately wished we could be together, but we couldn't even steal away to talk to each other on the phone. Leslie was always with Joan, and I was always with Rachel.

One afternoon at Joan's, we were almost caught. The four of us were playing with Joan's Ouija board, asking questions. Rachel and I wanted to know about the potential success of our record. But Leslie asked the board, "Have Chas and Joan ever kissed?"

"You guys know we have, so it's going to be 'yes,' " I said, trying to conceal my nervousness as Joan and I held onto the board.

Rachel changed the question: "Have they kissed *recently*?" We hadn't, but nonetheless the pointer defiantly indicated "yes."

"It's not true. We haven't!" Joan and I insisted.

But the Ouija board had more to say. It spelled out I-N-T-H-E-I-R-M-I-N-D-S.

Although we totally denied this pseudomystical revelation, a tremendous wave of suspicion and distrust washed over Leslie and Rachel. Because of a Ouija board! Rachel and I even talked about it later that night, but I denied it again and again. I was always full of denials then, hoping the subject would be pushed aside.

Not long after this incident, my feelings for Joan became almost unbearable. I really, really, *really* wanted to be with her. I knew it was over between Rachel and me, and I could barely tolerate having to be so dishonest.

Yet Rachel and I were about to achieve our dream and record an album. We'd worked so hard for this as a couple. It was our fantasy that a couple in love could make music together—not unlike what my parents had done. Even that day on the bridge in Paris, I had flashed on that. I sensed that Rachel, like my dad, could be the driving force in our pairing. Like my mom, I was the better singer but wasn't able to assert as much influence and power behind the scenes. Also, I was afraid to do music alone. That's how my parents had become a duo: My dad was supposed to just write the songs and produce the records rather than sing and be on stage, but my mom had such overwhelming stage fright that she insisted he go on stage with her. Rachel and I were a less extreme version of that scenario, but I still wanted her to be there with me, wanted her to be part of it, because I was really scared of the prospect of doing it myself. I knew instinctively that she'd be a really good motivator, and we were so ridiculously close that I didn't want to spend any time away from her.

But now, while the dream of making a record together was coming true, the fantasy of being partners in both love and music had become false. It would only take a week together in the studio before our relationship began to fall apart completely.

THREE

Our recording sessions started with great excitement. We'd chosen a studio at Capitol Records in Hollywood—the landmark round building with the phonograph needle rising from the top. We wanted to lay down the basic tracks in one of the big rooms there. The band that influenced us the most was the Beatles, and they had recorded for Capitol, so we wanted to recapture a similarly organic feeling of a large sound (especially from the drums) in a large room. Legends like Frank Sinatra had recorded in this studio too, so history was dripping off the walls.

The cool thing about the basic tracks was that we'd have all the musicians playing together, rather than having each instrument recorded separately. The musicians we were recording with were incredible, including the famous rock drummer Jim Keltner. They really seemed to like the music, which gave us a big boost because they were seasoned pros who'd worked on tons of albums.

Rachel and I weren't playing instruments at this point—we were just laying down "scratch" vocals with the tracks—but being in the booth with Rich, soaking it all in, thrilled us. We even documented everything with a camcorder. It was like a big party.

Our friends dropped by often, including Joan, Leslie, Amy, and Donna. In fact, there were so many people around that Rich didn't have a chance to be inappropriate with Rachel, so we all got along great. This was everything we'd been working for, finally coming together in harmonious collaboration.

Unfortunately, the perfection of the moment didn't last long.

I was still conflicted about the Joan-Rachel situation. One day when Amy visited the studio, I went off with her to a lounge and told her how hard it was to keep stuffing down my feelings, especially as my romance with Rachel had waned so drastically. Amy's advice was that I should sleep with Joan once, just to get it out of my system, and then everything could go back to normal with Rachel. I liked that idea a lot, since it would take care of all my needs. I really wanted to sleep with Joan, *and* I wanted everything to go back to normal, especially since I didn't want my life complicated by a painful breakup.

Still, I decided I had to break up with Rachel.

"I think our relationship has turned into a friendship and working relationship," I told her one night at home. "We should just acknowledge that, because it's reality." I didn't even mention my feelings for Joan. I just wanted to make a clean break with Rachel so that when I did get together with Joan—which was inevitable—I could tell Rachel that nothing had happened until after we'd broken up. The last thing I wanted was to cheat on her.

But surprise, surprise, it turned out that Rachel had already cheated on *me*. She confessed that a month before, when Joan had given a party for Rachel's birthday, the birthday girl had snuck outside to make out with our hairdresser! Amy had caught them together, but being superdiscrete she hadn't told me. Rachel also told me she had fooled around with our hairdresser a few times after the party, although they hadn't actually slept together.

She only told me about this dalliance after I suggested we break up, probably trying to shock me into changing my mind. She thought I was only talking about a breakup in an abstract way and that if I pictured it in concrete terms—such as her kissing our hairdresser—I wouldn't want to go ahead with it.

But I reacted in a completely different way—I laughed! I'd been pining over Joan but hadn't done anything more than hold hands with her, while Rachel had taken matters much further with another girl. Knowing this quickly relieved how guilty I'd been feeling.

Since I didn't react the way she'd expected, Rachel got really upset, begging me not to break up with her and insisting she was still in love with me. Besides, she said, what about our record?

"I need a week apart to think about things," I told her.

I decided to spend that week at Joan's, which would seem like throwing gasoline on the fire of Rachel's earlier suspicions. But strangely enough, in her misery about my desire to break up, Rachel's concerns about Joan somehow dissolved. She decided that whatever I needed in the next week was OK, as long as I changed my mind and stayed with her. I think she suspected something was going on, but she was probably in denial. She thought Joan was just a friend, and since Joan had two other girlfriends, how could she possibly fool around with me?

✳

Joan only lived about five minutes from our house, but I had a giddy feeling as I drove over there. I was so excited knowing the warm and enveloping welcome I'd receive.

Fortunately, Rachel and I had two days off from recording that week, so Joan and I had plenty of time to relax in each other's company. On our first day we went to the zoo, of all places. It was a weekday, and few people had come out to see the animals, so it was easy to hold hands or put our arms around each other. It was incredibly romantic. I wasn't even worried about being seen. Everything was so fresh and new with Joan; I was just amazed to be with her.

That night we went out for Japanese food, which was a favorite of ours. Again everything took on a romantic glow as we drank sake and held hands under the table. Back at the house that night, we sat on the couch and watched TV, with Joan sitting between my legs as I wrapped my arms around her. We hadn't kissed, because Joan was hesitant—nothing was squared away yet in my relationship with Rachel. But now I couldn't wait any longer. I turned her head toward me and at last kissed her. The kiss didn't disappoint in the slightest. *This isn't anything like kissing her when I was eighteen*, I thought. *This is much, much better.*

Joan hadn't changed significantly in the past four years, but I certainly had. I now felt very empowered. When I was younger, Joan had controlled everything between us because I was so timid. I was under her spell, vulnerable, overwhelmed by my feelings for her. Now I had the confidence to be in charge, to take her head in my hands and turn her lips toward mine. It felt good to kiss *her*, rather than the other way around. It was a long, passionate kiss, and she was totally there with me, totally responding to me. She had always blown my mind; now I was having a similar effect on her. I learned quickly that Joan liked being in a somewhat submissive role, allowing the other person to have a sexual power over her.

After we pulled apart, I said, "I'm sorry, but I just couldn't wait any longer."

"I'm glad you didn't," Joan smiled. "You've certainly changed since you were eighteen, Chas."

I kissed her again, with equal passion.

When we finally took a breath, Joan asked me if I wanted to go into the bedroom with her.

"I'd love to," I told her, "but I'm just not ready to make love with you. I'm not ready to betray my relationship with Rachel that way."

"I understand. I'll respect whatever you're comfortable with," Joan said.

Having spent so many nights as a guest at Joan's house, it was blissful to finally share her bed. We climbed in with our clothes on, both knowing what being naked would lead to, but despite our good intentions our shirts quickly came off. We stayed up most of the night, kissing and touching and holding each other. We stopped short of sex, though; I wasn't ready to take that final step. I needed that night of *not* having sex in order to have a clear conscience. Feeling so much passion for Joan made me know for sure that I wanted to take it further. I really, really wanted to make love with her, and now I was willing to risk my relationship with Rachel to have that intimacy.

The next day I returned to the studio, but that night Joan took me with her to a friend's party. She was supposed to meet Connie there and didn't want to cancel out. I wasn't altering my life with Rachel at this point, so Joan didn't want to alter her life for me either. Besides, she didn't want to rattle any cages with Connie or Leslie yet, because they were her birds in the hand, so to speak. Joan didn't like being alone, and a relationship with me remained an uncertainty.

We didn't want it to be obvious that something was transpiring between us, but it killed me that we couldn't be together. When we got to the party, I somehow maneuvered her into a bathroom, and we started making out. I was acting like a teenage boy; I wanted her so badly. I was halfway toward going all the way with her when she stopped me.

"The first time we make love," she said, "is *not* going to be in a bathroom."

When Connie arrived shortly after that, Joan greeted her with a hug and kiss. That only capped my frustration about not being with Joan, and I dealt with it by drinking so much white wine that I wouldn't be able to touch the stuff for years. Still, Joan and I cautiously flirted with each other throughout the evening. Any time Connie left the room, we exchanged deep, meaningful glances and mouthed things like "I want you so bad." As I got more and more plastered, my silent communication became even more graphic.

Yet that night Connie slept in Joan's bed, and I was

relegated to the back bedroom once again. *It's good that I'm drunk*, I thought.

The next morning, after Connie left for work, Joan retrieved me from the back bedroom and brought me to bed with her. Rachel and I had been given another day off, and it was to be my last one with Joan before my week of soul searching ended. Joan and I didn't have sex, much as we both would have liked, because she had other plans.

First we went out to breakfast in Toluca Lake, then to the fabulous Huntington Library and Gardens in Pasadena. We spent the day strolling through the lush grounds and having tea at a charming Japanese teahouse. After that, we found a bench in the middle of a forest of huge bamboo in the Japanese garden and sat there talking and kissing.

"This is so private it feels like we could make love right here and no one would notice," I said.

"It's certainly more romantic than my friend's bathroom floor," Joan smiled.

"I guess I got carried away. It's just that it's been building up for so long. I feel I'm ready now."

"Oh, you are, are you?" Joan raised an eyebrow.

I nodded enthusiastically.

"OK," said Joan, "then I propose a sex date."

"A sex date?" I was intrigued.

"When we leave here we'll go to the market and pick up a bottle of sake and the ingredients for linguine with clam sauce. We'll cook it together at my house. After we eat, we'll retire to the bedroom and—"

"And do what I've wanted to do with you since I was fourteen."

"Exactly."

With that decided, we quickly left the Japanese garden.

✳

Gelson's Market was right behind Joan's house in the Valley. While we shopped, Joan practiced some subtle foreplay in the produce section while no one was looking. For some reason, the produce section always made her frisky! We finally dragged ourselves and our groceries home and prepared the meal. Cooking took my mind off how nervous I felt about what was coming. We ate at Joan's bar, and between bites of linguini and sips of sake we could hardly keep our hands off each other. It was all so exciting and romantic—and stressful. *It's finally going to happen*, I thought. *Will it be what I've imagined? Will I be what Joan has imagined?* I knew Joan was a very sexual woman, and so much more experienced than I, so I was feeling performance anxiety on top of everything else.

After dinner we drifted toward the bedroom, where Joan lit dozens of candles. We immediately pulled each other close to kiss, then slowly took off each other's clothes. As I undressed Joan, I was taken aback—and unbelievably aroused—by the sight of the black lace lingerie she'd worn for me. Up to that point, I'd only been with high school girls, then with Rachel; I'd never been with an ultrafeminine, "real" woman who would wear something so erotic. Yet I'd always fantasized about making love with a woman wearing a garter belt and stockings—I guess I'd seen the movie *Bull Durham* too many times. Like Susan Sarandon in that film, Joan was completely comfortable with her body, uninhibited and extremely sensual. The sweet perfume on her baby-smooth skin added the final sensual touch. I was in heaven.

After all this time we were finally naked together in bed, arms and legs entangled, our lips locked in a deep kiss. With one hand I slowly explored her body, stopping to fondle her breast, while my other hand made its way down her stomach and between her legs. I teased her until I could no longer stand it and went inside, our bodies easily falling into a rhythm not unlike the dance we'd been doing around each other for so many years. She talked to me throughout, which I wasn't used to but found extremely exciting. As Joan quickly rose to a climax, she whispered to me the sexiest words I'd ever been told.

After she lay in my arms for several moments, we began to kiss again. Joan moved on top of me and kissed her way down my neck and to my breasts, where she softly licked, then sucked. She ran her tongue down my belly to her final destination, where she skillfully pleasured me so completely that it took my breath away. As I let go of all my pent-up feelings, I thought, *I can't believe this is happening...I can't believe this is Joan...I can't believe how good this feels.*

Needless to say, we didn't get much sleep that night. Being with Joan was completely different than being with Rachel—Joan was so uninhibited, so passionate, so talkative. I felt a little overwhelmed. I was surprised at how sexually aggressive Joan was, because she'd told me she'd been with a lot of old-school butch dykes who didn't want her to do *anything* to them. Joan was used to being on her back a lot, for lack of a better expression, and we even discussed this beforehand. I said, "That's not going to work for me." So I was surprised by what a great lover she was, especially at oral sex, which is something Rachel and I rarely engaged in. Joan went out of her way to make herself physically appealing, smelling good from head to toe. She was trimmed and shaved, soft, and immaculately groomed. Joan was like a courtesan: She knew just how to make her sexual partner feel comfortable and exactly how to turn her on.

It was all good, that night with Joan, but the next day I needed to process the experience. Had I just gotten something out of my system? Or was it more than that?

That morning, Rachel came to pick me up, because we only had one car. Joan was getting a massage when Rachel arrived, so I left without having a chance for much intimacy. I just kissed Joan on the cheek, whispered "I love you," and took off with Rachel to the studio.

Later that day we were recording something for which I used my acoustic guitar as a sort of percussion instrument, holding it like a cello between my legs and playing it like a drum. Suddenly I flashed to Joan's head being between my legs, and I experienced another electric surge. At that moment I realized I hadn't simply gotten my longtime sexual feelings for her out of my system. I definitely wanted to go there with her again and again. In a way I was disappointed. I had hoped I'd only have to sleep with Joan once, because our intense attraction was complicating my life.

I still couldn't decide what to do about Rachel. Our relationship clearly wasn't working, but instead of separating, we entered a kind of limbo. We weren't officially broken up, but we weren't much of a couple either. Rachel didn't want us to break up, and she kept begging me to stay, so I stayed. She also started to intimate that our breakup would have disastrous effects on our music career. Even Rachel's mom, a lovely Jewish mother who used to say things to like, "Why can't you girls just be good friends and find some nice boys?" called and asked me not to break up with her daughter.

"You're breaking Rachel's heart. What about the album? What about your career?" she said.

"We're going to be good friends," I told her, "just like you always wanted."

But still I tried to make it work with Rachel. When Joan dropped by the studio in subsequent weeks, I pretended to myself that I was over her. I even told her something to that effect one night at the studio.

"I'm starting to get you out of my system," I said stupidly.

She didn't know how to respond; I was so obviously insensitive to her feelings. I was so young then—I had gotten friendship and sex confused. I thought it was still OK to treat Joan like a friend and a confidante, even though I had become intimate with her. I should have realized that it was hurtful to tell her I didn't want to have feelings for her.

As Rachel and I were leaving for home that night, I spotted Joan's signature on the sign-in/sign-out list and just seeing it gave me a rush. *Fuck!* I thought. *I'm not over her after all. What the hell am I going to do?*

As soon as I got home, I snuck away to a phone and called Joan. "I don't know why I said that tonight," I apologized. "Of course I still have feelings for you."

"I'm glad, Chas," she said. "I definitely have feelings for you too. And I felt really sad when you told me that at the studio."

I felt chided and guilty for how I had acted. I realized I was just starting to learn how to treat a woman.

The week after Joan and I slept together was Thanksgiving. We were invited to Joan's for dinner, but two days before Rachel told me she didn't want to go.

"I'm so tired—I just want to stay home and relax with you," she said.

It certainly would *not* be relaxing for me if we didn't go to Joan's, because I would be the one cooking the turkey and all the fixings for Rachel (and Amy and Donna, who were also invited to Joan's). Besides, I had committed to making my famous ambrosia salad and helping Joan cook her feast. But beneath all those reasons, I just wanted to be with Joan.

"It would be rude if we didn't go," I said. "I promised I'd help Joan."

Rachel immediately got pissed off. "It's always about Joan. You'd drop everything for Joan. I feel like I don't even matter anymore."

"It doesn't have anything to do with Joan," I said, half-believing my own excuses. "I wouldn't do that to anybody so soon before Thanksgiving. It wouldn't be good manners."

"Fine, Chas, we'll go to Joan's. But next time we do what I want to do."

On Thanksgiving Day, I left early for Joan's, bringing the salad ingredients. Before Rachel arrived, Joan and I were able to sneak over to Scotti's a couple of times on some pretense and find a secret corner in which to kiss. We almost got caught, though, when Rachel came over to Scotti's, and for the rest of the night I felt very uncomfortable. I may have been projecting, but I imagined that all three of us were uncomfortable all evening long. The only thing I found to be thankful for was that Joan and I hadn't gotten caught. I felt very much in the middle, trying to keep both these women happy, which of course was impossible. I was trying not to rock the boat with Rachel, so I was keeping everything with Joan under wraps. It was the most acting I'd done since high school.

※

December was horrible. Rich had started making suggestive comments to Rachel again and demanded that she always sit close to him at the mixing board. He didn't cross the line of inappropriate touching, but he often touched her arm or her leg, or put his arm around her, far more than she wanted. If she didn't respond to his liking—if she didn't sit right next to him or flirt back—or if she expressed annoyance at his comments, he'd shut down and we wouldn't be able to get any work done. Rachel was miserable. Not only were things rocky between us, but this crazy producer was making her life hell. The pressure all seemed to rest on her: Could she play along with Rich without compromising herself? We thought that the album's success rested on her ability to answer "yes."

For our Christmas break, Rachel made plans to go to Long Island to be with her family, while I decided to spend time with my mom and our family in Aspen. It was the first holiday Rachel and I had spent apart since we'd gotten together, so we knew things between us were awry. But we also planned, as was our tradition, to meet up in San Francisco on New Year's Eve to see the Grateful Dead.

I arranged it so that I wouldn't leave for Aspen until

a day after Rachel flew to New York. After I dropped her off at the airport, I headed straight for Joan's. I was dying to be with her again. Since that week at her house, I hadn't been able to catch more than a few brief moments with her. That night, we went out for Japanese food and couldn't keep our hands apart or take our eyes off each other. Joan had the most beautiful eyes of anyone I've ever been with—intensely blue, sparkling, wide and expressive. I called her "Bright Eyes." All the beautiful parts of her character shone from them.

"I can't believe we're finally alone together," I told her.

"I know," Joan smiled. She hadn't been in the same hell as me; her life had continued along. But I knew she wanted to be with me.

"It's so hard to see you at the studio with everyone else around—it's torture to look but not touch," I said.

Joan giggled sweetly and squeezed my hand under the table.

"You know how badly I want to be with you, baby, don't you?"

Joan nodded. "I know."

"I feel like I'm going crazy. Everything in the studio has gotten so bad. Rich has been relentless with Rachel. I can't tell you how much time we've wasted while he throws temper tantrums. The tension gets unbearable. On top of that, anytime I try to talk to Rachel about breaking up, or me moving out, she won't hear of it. She immediately says she can't work with me if I break up with her. And I'm starting to feel guilty about what I'm putting *you* through."

"You're under enough pressure," she said with an understanding look. "I'm not going to add to that. I want the time we spend together to be about having fun and enjoying each other."

"Thank you." I caressed both her hands. "You're an angel."

"We'll have our time together, if it's meant to be. I understand you need to concentrate on your career right now," Joan told me.

With that I relaxed, and we slipped into a conversation about just how glad we were to be together, even for just a night.

But when we left the restaurant and got back to Joan's house, we encountered another episode of dyke drama: Leslie had been snooping around. There was a message on Joan's machine from Les saying she had looked in Joan's window and spotted a suitcase in the front hall. *Who was there, and why?* she wanted to know. Perhaps she suspected it was me but didn't know for sure because my car wasn't there. (Joan had picked me up at my place, since she planned to take me to the airport the next day.)

As I've said, Joan's relationship with Leslie had been full of such dramatic episodes. Les had even busted in on Joan when she'd been with other women. Joan had nick-named her "the private dick" and "Clouseau" because of her spying, and joked that she'd carved a permanent groove in the road in front of Joan's house from driving by to check on her. Even though Les accepted the terms of a nonmonogamous relationship, she still could become consumed with jealousy—and Joan continued to put up with her snooping and jealous fits.

Joan came up with some excuse about the suitcase, but we were afraid that Les would come by anyway. In the past she'd broken into the house through the sliding glass doors in Joan's bedroom. Joan realized that Leslie didn't fully buy whatever story she told her, and knew how relentless Leslie could be if she thought Joan was withholding something.

Considering the circumstances, we decided to spend the night at Scotti's. Les was afraid of Scotti because Scotti wouldn't tolerate her bullshit. She also wanted to stay on Scotti's good side, because she knew how important she was to Joan. Scotti knew about Joan and me at that point, because we had confided in her. She was mostly supportive, but she was also worried what my mom would think. Scotti had this blind loyalty to my mom. I think her fear was that if my mom got upset, she'd turn her anger on Scotti and demand, "How could you let this happen?!" Her fear wasn't based in reality, however. My mom would never have gotten pissed off at Scotti about this; that wasn't her style at all.

It was nerve-wracking to spend the night at Scotti's, since Joan and I wanted to make love and we had to keep the noise down. Still, our second time together sexually proved to be much easier for me. My reservations had vanished, Joan's sexual openness didn't intimidate me this time, and I knew, without a doubt, that I wanted to be with her.

✳

The next day I flew to Aspen. During that week, I talked to Joan on the phone a lot—which was wonderful, since I hadn't been able to talk with her on the phone in Los Angeles unless I snuck into Amy's room or into an empty room at the studio. I was also dying to tell someone in Aspen what was going on, so I chose my Aunt Gee (Georgeann), my mom's sister, who'd always been supportive of me. I told her I was having an affair with someone I liked a lot, but I didn't mention a name. Just as I was about to tell her it was Joan, she stopped me.

"I think I know who it is, so you don't have to tell me," Gee said. "In fact, I don't want you to tell me until you talk about it with your mom."

I wasn't ready to tell my mom. We weren't having the kind of relationship where we talked about those kind of things. Besides, although she was totally accepting of me being gay, she still wasn't completely comfortable with it. But at the time, I wasn't completely comfortable being gay either and probably projected my feelings onto her. I figured that I didn't really need to tell her until Joan and I had actually become a couple, and I didn't think that would be anytime soon.

Without using Joan's name, I told Gee everything that was going on. I described how I felt that I had to stay with Rachel because of the album, even though I'd fallen in love with someone else. My aunt just listened, as she always had, and that comforted me somewhat.

At the end of the week I returned to Los Angeles. I'd worked it out so I'd be there a day before I had to drive up to San Francisco, so I could grab another day alone with Joan. This time we stayed, unbothered, at her house. I didn't bring my car with me, so Leslie couldn't know I was there, and we closed all the blinds so she couldn't peer in.

Very early the next morning, I headed north with Amy on California's Interstate 5, even though we'd have to encounter a horrible storm on the mountain pass known as The Grapevine. We hardly noticed it, as I talked Amy's ear off about everything that was going on. I knew she felt stuck in the middle between her two friends, but she never broke either of our confidences. She understood how bad the ramifications would be if Rachel found out about Joan and me.

Rachel met us at the hotel in San Francisco where she and I had fallen in love years before. She was probably thinking that, given our history, San Francisco was the one place where we could start getting our relationship back on track. We'd always had such a good time there. She'd even bought me great presents for Christmas, including obscure percussion instruments from around the world that she found in a store in New York. But her generosity made me feel horrible, especially since I was keeping up a false front with her. I'd just spent two glorious nights with Joan during the past week; I was completely gone from Rachel as a romantic partner, and I couldn't go back.

I felt guilty the entire time we were in San Francisco, especially since it hit me how much Rachel still loved and cared for me. I had come to believe that she only wanted to be with me because we'd been together so long, or because her ego couldn't accept that I had initiated the breakup. But in San Francisco I realized that she was willing to go out of her way for me—which was unusual, because she had always expected things to be done for her. She was now making an effort to woo me, but I could no longer be wooed by her. I now started to believe that not only would I wreck our career if we broke up, but I'd break her heart as well. That was a hard one for me, because I hate to cause someone else pain.

Rachel and I went to several Dead shows in San Francisco, and at the New Year's Eve show, around midnight, I had the first anxiety attack of my life. At first I thought I'd accidentally been given LSD. I got a big knot in my stomach and felt a tightening in my chest. I almost felt like my *clothes* were tightening.

"Rachel, I think somebody dosed my drink," I said. I had been drinking Diet Coke from a paper cup, and I'd often worried about having my drink spiked with acid at a Dead show. I had never tried the drug, because I had gotten paranoid just from smoking pot. "I'm feeling really weird. My stomach feels like it has bad butterflies, and my heart is racing."

"Who would have dosed you?" Rachel replied, only mildly concerned.

"I don't know, someone in the row behind us?" I had put my drink down on the floor under my seat and pushed it way back so that I wouldn't kick it over.

"Doesn't sound like you were dosed, Chas. It sounds like you're having an anxiety attack." Rachel was a little annoyed, because she knew I didn't want to be there with her at the show. Nonetheless, she wanted to help me. "Just try to relax, take some deep breaths," she said. "I promise you'll feel better in no time."

As time passed and I didn't feel any worse, I realized it wasn't acid, and I started to relax. If nothing else, Rachel had proven she was still a good friend.

My anxiety, I realized, was just a manifestation of the stress and turmoil in my life. I was living a lie with Rachel, and if I stayed with her, all I could imagine was pain. Then again, what if I left her? Just more pain.

✳

It's hard to believe, but after we returned from San Francisco, Rachel and I resumed our dysfunctional life together. Our sex life was pretty much nil, but we still acted at being together.

We were still making the never-ending album, but at least we had one thrilling experience during that time: We got to record with Jerry Garcia of the Grateful Dead.

Rachel and I had met Jerry around the time we'd met Bob Weir, hanging out backstage at a Dead concert. We had given our first demo tape to Bob because he felt more accessible, but maybe that was just in our minds. Jerry, after all, was JERRY GARCIA, and we didn't feel we could call him up or ask him to listen to our demo or hang out with him in New York, as we did with Bobby. We did visit with him backstage whenever the Dead played New York (we would go to every show), and once I said to him, "So Jerry, when we get a deal, would you play on our record?" He said, "Sure," perhaps thinking I was joking—but I wasn't.

During the Dead's New Year's shows, I decided to pop the question to him again. "We're in the middle of doing our record, Jerry—would you still be willing to play on a couple of songs?" He immediately said yes and seemed really happy for us. After that, it was just a matter of working out our schedules.

Finally, in the spring, Rachel and Rich and I flew up to San Francisco, then rented a car and drove down to the Dead's warehouse-like studio in the mountains of Palo Alto. This was a dream come true for Rachel, since she'd been following the band religiously since high school. For Deadheads like her, the band itself was a religion, since she found insight and inspiration in their lyrics and improvisational playing. She didn't think of Jerry as a god exactly, but she found him to be God-inspired.

Jerry arrived late, dressed in his uniform of a black T-shirt, jeans, and sneakers. He seemed to be in a great mood. We played him some of our favorite cuts from the album so he could get a feel for our music, and then we played the two songs for which we wanted him to contribute guitar solos. Rich then plugged his guitar directly into the recording "board" (instead of miking his amp), and we sat around the board with him as he did four hours worth of takes. We all got such a kick out of being so close with Jerry, making music together.

Rich was on his best behavior that day. He hadn't met Jerry before, but they totally hit it off. He was charming and funny—men usually just saw Rich's good side. He did a good job producing as well, making Jerry's guitar riffs fit right into our songs, even if it wasn't the most logical combination. Jerry didn't play perfectly or slickly, so Rich ended up piecing together his solos from different takes, and in the end it sounded terrific.

Back in L.A., Joan still visited us regularly at the studio, along with our other friends. I was still afraid to leave Rachel. I'd been with her since I was eighteen, I'd grown up with her; it had always been ChasandRachel, one word. Whenever I tried to break away from her, she'd reel me back in. I kept leaving her a glimmer of hope that we'd work things out. It was maddening for both of us—I knew I was driving her just as crazy as she was driving me.

When I first told Rachel I wanted to end our relationship, I was very clear about my feelings and expected her to feel the same. We would just be admitting a truth that we already knew. But when she reacted the way she did, and we moved into an ongoing state of limbo, I started to doubt my feelings and it became more difficult for me to make the final break. Rachel wasn't making it any easier, because she didn't want to lose me. In addition, she began to make it very clear that she had no intention of continuing to work with me if I ended things with her. Bottom line, I was scared—scared that a breakup would make a huge change in my life and my career and that I'd lose the very significant connection I had with Rachel. I didn't want to lose the things I loved about her, especially our intellectual rapport. She's very smart, and although I didn't realize it then, I'm smart too. We talked about all sorts of things, sparring over different issues. It was the kind of rapport I didn't have with Joan. Joan wasn't intellectual, but she was wise in a worldly way. She didn't dispense pearls of wisdom about life—she was never preachy—but there was such a serenity about her that it became its own sort of wisdom. From Joan I got devoted, uncomplicated love, but I also craved the sort of stimulation I got from Rachel.

So I stayed with Rachel but continued my secret affair with Joan. It wasn't that hard to grab time with her—I'd just tell Rachel that I needed some space and that I was going to stay overnight at my best friend Joan's house. Rachel suspected something was going on and asked me about it all the time, but I'd just say, "No no no no no." I truly believed Rachel couldn't handle the truth. I still planned to split up with her, and then after we'd been broken up for a while I'd tell her that Joan and I had just then gotten together. But my plan wasn't working, because I wasn't making the breakup happen. I got anxiety attacks sometimes when I was with Joan, because ending things with Rachel scared me to death.

These months were a blur; I just know it was a miserable time. Rachel and I were in the studio six days a week, dealing with Rich and his manipulations. Rachel was under much more pressure than me, because she had to sit by Rich's side every second or he'd stop working. She made the best of it by trying to gain as much knowledge from him as she could. When he wasn't throwing a temper tantrum, they managed to maintain a strong musical collaboration, and she was a sponge, soaking up anything she could about music and production.

But the toxic work environment was murder on everyone's relationship—the marriages of both Rich and our engineer Peter Coleman broke up as well. We joked with the assistant engineer that he'd better get another job or say goodbye to his girlfriend.

For me, the musical experience had become awful, since I'd been pushed out of the way. Rich was obsessed with Rachel, not me, and after a while I felt like it was just their record. Unless I felt adamant about something, I kept my mouth shut. Everything had become a fight, and I didn't have any fight left in me.

When the time came for us to record our lead vocals, Rich refused to interact with Rachel and me at all. It was already a strange situation, because he'd waited until the very end of the recording process before letting us lay down those tracks. Meanwhile, he hired himself and his brothers (they'd had a singing group together) and his friends to cut background vocals. To justify why those harmonies took so long and cost so much, he made up the excuse that he needed a lot of backup because "Chas and Rachel are scared their voices aren't strong enough." He told that lie to my mother as well as the record company. Aside from the blatant disrespect, Rachel and I had to match our lead vocals to the background harmonies, rather than the other way around.

When we finally started recording our vocal parts, Rich wouldn't give us any direction other than a curt, "Do it again." He'd say that over and over and over without explaining what he was looking for. This was the first time Rachel and I had ever made a record, so we were vulnerable and needed guidance. Rich had given us much more direction when we did our demos; now he was acting like he didn't give a damn and seemed to hardly be listening. He had us by the balls, so to speak, and was playing it to the hilt.

At that point, we'd had it. At the most important part of the recording process, he was treating it like it was *nothing.* Since all the instrumental tracks were completed, Rachel and I finally decided we didn't need him anymore. One day we just walked out of the studio, making it clear that we wouldn't show up the next day.

We went to see John Kalodner at Geffen Records to tell him what had been going on—how Rich had been wasting studio time while acting disrespectfully toward us. Kalodner told us to fire him and let our engineer Peter—who had produced the Knack's big hit "My Sharona"—finish the album for us. We finally saw a way to take back our power.

But it turned out that Rich didn't want to leave the project. He was scared and upset about this turn of events, and asked John if we could all talk. We agreed, and the next day at the studio the three of us sat down with John, his assistant Deborah, and my mom's manager, Bumper, who was best friends with Rich and had probably been called by him to help smooth things over. Eager to keep the job, Rich promised he'd act appropriately from now on—though I don't remember him apologizing for his past behavior. Rachel and I realized that we should have threatened to fire him long before this, since the threat was the only thing that had registered. Only when he was about to lose the reins of the album he'd worked so long and hard on did the humble Rich suddenly appear.

Rachel and I decided to give him another chance. We had nothing to lose, because we could always fire him if he reneged on his word. So we completed the vocal tracks over the next couple of weeks with Rich at the controls, and he was an absolute prince, acting as if nothing bad had ever happened between us. We got the good Rich Matthews again, and when he was good he was great. That's what was so frustrating about him: He could be the funniest, most talented person you'd ever met—or the meanest, nastiest prick in the universe.

✳

In June, while we were still recording lead vocals, Joan left Los Angeles to spend six weeks in Maui, where Scotti had a condo. I'd been spending more and more time at Joan's house, and when she left I decided to stay there full-time. It was harder than ever to be with Rachel, especially since she was now drinking heavily. It was probably even more upsetting to her that I was staying at Joan's when Joan wasn't there, because it showed her that I just didn't want to be around her, whether or not Joan was in the picture.

Rachel and I had somehow made a nonverbal agreement that we wouldn't make any big changes in our lives until the record was done. I was there physically, but emotionally I had shut down from her completely. It would have been much easier for us to break up, mourn the loss, and move on.

Rachel drank more and more to relieve the pain of the situation, and her drinking ultimately made things worse. She was getting drunk every day that we weren't working, and when she drank she acted pretty crazy and careless. One night when I was at Joan's house, Rachel went out drinking with Amy and Donna. When she got home, very drunk, she accidentally put her hand through the glass of our bedroom door and sliced it badly. Amy asked me to meet them at the emergency room, and I did. I couldn't set any reasonable boundaries. I'd rush back to Rachel whenever she asked me to.

On another particularly awful day, while Joan was in Hawaii, Rachel showed up drunk at seven A.M. at Joan's house, where I was staying. She knocked on the door and I let her in.

"Can I play this for you?" she asked, holding up a tape. She said she'd been up all night with Rich recording a version of the Stevie Wonder song "Blame It on the Sun." It's about a breakup in which the person tries blame the situation on everyone but herself, but finally realizes she's the one to blame.

"Sure," I told her, and she put the tape into the stereo. Both the instrumentation and Rachel's singing were very emotional, almost heart-wrenching. I felt horrible listening to it, because I knew a song couldn't change the way I felt.

"It's beautiful," I told her when the song ended. "Your vocals are really great."

"Thanks," she said, smiling, and took my hand. "Chas, will you come home with me?"

"No," I said.

I wasn't sure whether Rachel was still in love with me or just afraid of being alone. I only knew that I was trying to stave off our final breakup because she was constantly threatening that she'd no longer work with me if our relationship ended. She even went so far in her drunken rages as to say that if we broke up, she'd call our record company and tell them things that might sabotage my music career. She never clarified what those "things" were, but still her threats held weight for me.

I knew I was handling things horribly, even though I tried to convince myself that I was doing this *for* Rachel. Instead I was emotionally torturing her. For the sake of my career, I thought I could keep up a facade. Then again, I wasn't willing to cut off my relationship with Joan. If I had, I would have been beyond miserable. The only thing that kept me together through this ordeal was my relationship with Joan. Without her, I would have been like Rachel, deeply depressed and almost losing my mind. Joan, amazingly enough, accepted my comings and goings during this period, but I knew she wouldn't put up with it forever. She told me so. She said I'd eventually have to break up with Rachel or she'd call a halt to our relationship. Joan didn't believe that Rachel would stop working with me if I ended the relationship, saying the record deal meant too much to her for her to do that.

*

After we finished the vocals, Rich and Peter started mixing the album. They'd do a rough mix of a song, then have Rachel and me listen to it and help them tweak it. By this time, the pressure had eased a lot. Since Rich was being less obnoxious, Rachel started to feel closer to him again, and he provided an ego boost for her. She felt so stripped down and rejected by me, yet Rich kept building her up, telling her how beautiful and talented she was. He even bought her a brand new Martin, the Rolls Royce of acoustic guitars.

After the mix came the mastering of the album, but before that started we were given a week off. Rachel decided to visit her family in New York. "In that case, I'm going to Hawaii to meet Joan," I told her. Joan had been away a few weeks, and I missed her like crazy. I couldn't even talk to her much on the phone, because both Leslie and Connie had been in Hawaii visiting her— at different times, of course.

Rachel wasn't thrilled with my plans, but she didn't give me as hard a time as I'd expected. Perhaps she thought I wasn't serious about going. Anyway, I was still lying about my motivation. "This is my best friend and she's got a place in Maui where I can stay for a week— why *wouldn't* I go?" I was lying to all my friends about Joan, except for Amy and Scotti. My other friends were all Rachel's as well, and they would have run off and told her.

On the flight to Hawaii, even though I was seated in the midst of a noisy family, I was calm as could be. I was escaping my crazy life in Los Angeles for an entire week.

I could have floated the plane there, I was so happy.

From the moment I stepped out into the open-air Maui Airport, feeling the trade winds and smelling the intensely aromatic island flowers, I was in paradise. Joan was supposed to meet me in baggage claim, but I didn't spot her at first. I scanned an ocean of people, and suddenly the ocean parted and there she was. I had wondered if I was building her up too much in my mind and if the reality wouldn't match my imagination, but I wasn't disappointed at all. Joan looked even more gorgeous than I'd remembered. The Hawaiian humidity had curled her hair, and I loved that look on her. We hugged and kissed and whispered how much we'd missed each other, and then Joan gave me a lei.

"Welcome to Hawaii," she said with her sweetest smile. Then she added the old joke, "Now you can say you got lei'd at the airport." She knew I didn't like most flowers, but this was a lei of interwoven leaves that was traditionally worn by Hawaiian kings—and it made *me* feel like a king.

The entire ride back from the airport to the condo, I couldn't take my eyes off Joan or stop touching her as we talked about all the things we'd do on the island together. There was no longer any awkwardness between us; it was as if we'd never been apart. Joan's friend Jeannie was with us too, but I immediately felt comfortable with her.

At the condo, Joan showered me with presents from the local surf shop—bathing suits, shorts, tank tops—all individually wrapped and placed on the bed. That was just so *Joan*, always thoughtful and giving. After I opened all the presents, we closed ourselves off in the bedroom and spent the afternoon making love—which was more amazing than I could have imagined.

That night, Joan wanted to take me to a typically Hawaiian place, so we went for dinner with a couple of her friends at the Grand Wailea Hotel. The restaurant has the tongue-twisting name Humuhumunukunuku-apua'a— after the Hawaiian fish—and it's a charming open-air, thatched-roof place situated on a lagoon. Joan ordered us a traditional fruity rum drink in a goblet the size of a pasta bowl, which we couldn't finish even though we shared it.

Our week in Hawaii was blissful; for me it felt like a love affair with both Joan and Hawaii. Joan knew the island well from her many trips there and loved to show it off. Besides Jeannie, Joan's friend Lauren, whom I already knew, also stayed with us in the two-bedroom condo, and we all got along great. It was the longest time I'd spent with Joan without our lovers interrupting.

We spent our days sunbathing and boogie-boarding, drinking cocktails at sunset in the condo, then going to a fabulous restaurant every night. One night we even went to a karaoke bar, though I was far too paranoid to get up and sing. It wasn't just that I was afraid of being recognized: When you're a professional musician you get used to having great sound behind you, and in comparison a rinky-dink karaoke machine is pretty frightening. Actually I did sing that night: While Jeannie, a professional singer, performed "Crazy," I sang along in Joan's ear. Joan always loved when I sang just to her.

I'd never been much of a beach person, but I started to become one. Every day, Joan packed a cooler with sodas and snacks and we headed for a different beach, each more spectacular than the last. My favorite was "little beach" in Makena, part of the larger Makena Beach, a huge expanse of creamy, fine sand. To the right of it, on the other side of a cliff that jutted over the ocean, was a smaller beach that catered to a gay, nude (we kept our clothes on), and boogie-boarding crowd. I'd never boogie-boarded before, even though my mom had a house in Malibu, but I guess that's because I hated the cold water of the ocean around Los Angeles. In Hawaii's warm water I quickly grew to love the sport. Joan loved boogie-boarding too. She may have been extremely feminine, but she was tremendously athletic as well—not the type who worried about getting her hair wet or looking less than perfect.

At one point we were boogie-boarding with a group of local teenage boys, and one big wave wiped me out quite dramatically. When I got up, Joan was about twenty yards behind me, furiously pointing at her chest. I couldn't figure out what she was doing. *Perhaps she's just trying to be funny*, I thought, *or showing off her bathing suit top*. Then I noticed the locals looking at me and laughing. I looked down and realized my bathing suit top had slid off, totally exposing my chest.

One night we dined out, just the two of us, at Joan's favorite restaurant in Maui—a romantic waterside Italian place in Wailea called Correlli's. Oddly enough, she had recently discovered that the maître d' was her long-lost boyfriend to whom she'd lost her virginity before he went off to Vietnam. Correlli's had a *mangia* bar near the kitchen, with a brick pizza oven, and that was Joan's favorite place to sit. There she could watch the chefs prepare their fabulous steamed clams in butter, garlic, and wine and try to figure out the recipe. We made mental notes of the ingredients as we ate, planning to try it for ourselves when we got home.

I rarely thought about the age gap between Joan and me, but occasionally it came up in the most unexpected ways. We had a Mexican lunch one afternoon in Makawao, a tiny mountain town where Hawaiian cowboys hang out. We'd just come from Paio beach and I was wearing a baseball hat. When the waitress came over to the table she brought a coloring book and crayons, but after she took our order—mostly appetizers and shots of tequila—she took the book and crayons away. Joan and I exchanged a look that said, *That's weird. Why did she bring it in the first place?* When we asked her about it, she looked at me and said, "I thought you were younger."

"How young? It's a children's coloring book!"

"Oh, eleven or twelve," she told me.

I was twenty-three years old and five foot six! After that, perhaps because she was embarrassed, she didn't even card me for the tequila. That sort of stuff happened a lot. It was pretty funny to me, but I think it secretly bothered Joan.

Our age couldn't keep us apart, though, because we were too good a match. We loved being together, just taking joy in pleasing each other. We trusted each other completely and knew that neither would intentionally hurt the other. Even though Joan was older, she wasn't jaded, and even though I was younger she appreciated the depth of my love for her. She told me I had made her *feel* again and that she loved my smile and how muscular I was. (She didn't like scrawny women; she said she appreciated a more masculine woman's physique.) During that week, we talked a lot about being together in the near future. It was certainly our understanding that there would be a future for us; it was only a matter of when.

The only sour note during our time together was the incessant phone calls I got from Rachel, which started the day after I arrived. Donna—Rachel's ex and now one of her best friends—had completely misinterpreted something I had told her when she drove me to the airport in Los Angeles.

"I'll bet you're really looking forward to this trip," she'd said to me.

"That's for sure," I replied. "I'll probably never want to come back."

I'd meant that I might never want to come back from the beauty of Hawaii, and I'd said it tongue in cheek. But when Donna repeated our conversation to Rachel, it came out as if I'd been serious about never wanting to come home.

So Rachel called me in Hawaii the next day. "What's this about you not wanting to come back?" she nearly screamed. She had good reason to be paranoid, of course, but she was acting a bit crazy. After that, she called every day just to let me know how freaked out she was about my being there. We had screaming fights, and I was afraid to hang up on her—I irrationally thought that if I didn't put up with everything she dumped on me, our lives and careers would fall apart. I was unbelievably insecure. Our fights would go on so long that I occasionally held up our group from going out. I was certainly wrong about how understanding Rachel had been about me going to Hawaii.

Before I had left for the islands, Rachel had been pumping Lauren for information about Joan and me. I flat-out lied to Lauren about it when she had asked.

"You've got to talk to Rachel, because there's *nothing* going on," I'd told her with a straight face. Now, being with Lauren in Hawaii, I took her aside and admitted the truth. Fortunately for me, her loyalty was to Joan, not Rachel, so she kept my secret. Not only did she keep it, but she thanked me for having lied to her up to that point, because it put her in a position where she didn't have to lie to Rachel.

Joan remained incredibly patient about the situation, even when Rachel and I had our long, drawn-out calls. But on our last day together, Joan taught me a big lesson. I'd been arguing on the phone with Rachel for about forty-five minutes when Joan finally said, "We're leaving now. You want to get off the phone?"

I showed no signs of ending the conversation. "No?" Joan said. "OK, see you later." With that, she and Jeannie left the condo. For Joan to do that on my last day with her in Hawaii was a ballsy move, but that's how she was. Joan would take something for as long as she could, then take action. We didn't get into many fights, and the few fights we did have were usually about Rachel.

By the time Joan returned, I was like a child in a corner, whimpering apologies. But Joan didn't want to talk about the incident at all; she had made her point by leaving, and she immediately let her anger go.

"Are you ready to go out now?" she simply asked.

"I'm really sorry," I told her.

"It's over," she said. "Now let's go out and enjoy the rest of the time you have here."

It was a relief for me to be with someone who just quietly acted on her annoyance, rather than someone who was a verbal fighter like Rachel. In Rachel's family there

would be frequent outpourings of overdramatic emotion—screaming! yelling!—and then it would be over.
There wasn't a lot of grudge-holding. They'd be fine and
laughing after a fight. When Rachel fought with me,
she'd get loud and angry and verbally hit below the belt,
then later say she didn't really mean it.

But I would feel crushed. When I was growing up, my
family never aired our feelings in a loud manner, and I
never went against the "rules." My instinct was not to
make any waves. I remember one vacation with my dad
in Lake Tahoe, when I was eight or so, when I accidentally broke a glass in the hotel bathroom. I was terrified
of getting in trouble, even though my dad rarely got upset
with me. So I wrapped the glass in toilet paper and hid it
in the trash. I don't know why I was like that, because I
don't remember anything in my early childhood that
might have triggered it. The only person who ever got
angry with me was our nanny, Clarice, but I was a pleas-
er even before she came to work for us. I hated con-
frontation, and I hated people being angry with me. I
still don't deal with anger well—mine or others. Maybe
it's because there were no healthy displays of anger in my
house. When my mom got angry, although it was rare,
she'd just shut down and be really cold, which terrified
me. I'd only seen my mom cry once, and it took a lot to
make me cry as well. Any show of emotion made me
uncomfortable, because my family was so buttoned up.
That's why I was more at ease with Joan's version of
anger—she'd just act hurt and upset—rather than yell like
Rachel. I could just feel guilty when Joan got mad at me.
Still, I left Hawaii on a good note with her.

"God, I wish I didn't have to leave," I said.

"I know, baby, so do I."

After the great week I'd had, and the awful trans-Pacific conversations with Rachel, the thought of returning to Los Angeles wasn't pleasant. It was really hard to get on the plane—it felt like I was flying into an inferno. Rachel was furious with me, and it wouldn't be pretty when I saw her again.

The only good thing I could think of was that Joan would only be in Hawaii another ten days. Then she'd return to Los Angeles, and we could steal some time together again.

FOUR

When I got back to Los Angeles, it was time to master our album, the final step in the recording process when all the sounds get balanced. Mastering is like putting the music through a polisher, and since it's mainly a technical process, Rachel and I didn't have much input other than saying, "That's good," "That's bad," "Add some bottom," or "Make it crisper."

The record sounded good to us—a sort of Beatles-meet-the-Bangles, hook-filled pop sound, with my higher voice blending well with Rachel's deeper one—but we'd lost all objectivity. Our biggest concern was that it had been overproduced; perhaps there was too much of everything, both vocally and instrumentally. The climate in the record business was changing right before our eyes and ears. When we came up with the concept for the album, we were in the late '80s/early '90s era of heavy metal glam "hair" bands, like Bon Jovi, Whitesnake, Def Leppard, and Cinderella, and we thought we could carve out a niche somewhere between that sort of rock and a straight pop sound. We wanted to be edgy but accessible. What we weren't banking on was the explosion created by Nirvana in 1991 with their album *Nevermind*. Grunge bands like Nirvana and Pearl Jam became the real alternative to the hair bands. We weren't nearly alternative enough.

We started to realize the problem while we were still mixing, and wondered whether the new "alternative" radio stations would be turned off because of all the strings we had, or whether pure pop stations would be turned off because of the guitars. Who would play our music? Our new rock-oriented manager Doc McGhee, who also handled Bon Jovi, Mötley Crüe, and Skid Row, helped us realize just how overproduced everything was. So we decided to remix a few of the songs we thought had potential as singles, scaling down the instrumentation. Not surprisingly, Rich didn't agree that we should do this, and that caused yet another big fight. But at this point I was just relieved to be getting the record over with. I still felt excited at the prospect of beginning my music career, which I was sure would be successful. The idea of failing never crossed my mind.

When we finished mastering, the record company loved what we turned in. As we were trying to choose a first single to release, they told us, "You've got so many hits on this record we don't know which one to pick!" (Later, when that first single tanked, we heard, "There are *no* hit singles on this record.") Even though we had a lot of work ahead of us, I imagined it would be easier than making the record had been. At least we wouldn't have to keep putting in twelve-hour days, and we could finally escape the sick environment the studio had turned into.

Because we were going to sell ourselves as a band, rather than just promote Rachel and myself, we had to actually put a band together. The record was extremely complex musically—we used horns, a twenty-four-piece orchestra on certain cuts, even bagpipes. We wanted to put in every whistle and bell we could. But now we faced the problem of reproducing those sounds on stage with a relatively small, six-piece unit consisting of drums, bass, lead guitar, keyboards, and Rachel and me on acoustic rhythm guitars. It was crunch time, so—if you can believe it—we hired Rich again to help us. Our dependency upon him was insane. We didn't think we were capable of doing any of this ourselves, and we didn't believe anyone else understood our music. He was our George Martin.

We held band auditions that August, and it was a grueling process. It had been difficult enough in New York, when we were living on a shoestring budget, to find musicians we liked, yet with much more money and resources at our disposal in Los Angeles it seemed just as difficult. There weren't that many good musicians on the West Coast who also had the look we were striving for. It boggled our minds. We weren't even judging the candidates for compatible personalities, because you can't tell that right away anyway. We just assumed the band we picked would be full of peace, love, happiness, and rock 'n' roll—all the stuff we'd found in New York. Man, were we wrong.

✳

After Joan returned from Hawaii, I stayed at her house almost all the time. Rachel was still drinking excessively, and I didn't want to be around her. Much to my relief, though, she'd started to date. We were unofficially broken up, so it wasn't like she was cheating on me. We had an agreement that we could both see other people, though I was a lot more comfortable with her dating someone than she would have been if she had known I was. I still didn't feel I could tell her about Joan, because it might have pushed her over the edge.

Nonetheless, Rachel kept trying to patch things up between us, and she used the opportunity of yet another mishap to lure me back once again. One night in September, she went out to dinner with Donna, Amy, and Sheila (a high school friend of mine she had gotten to know). They were all drinking a lot, and Rachel and Sheila started flirting with each other. They left the restaurant together and took a romantic walk on the beach, then headed back to Sheila's place in West Hollywood. They were both drunk and shouldn't have been driving. Plus, Sheila, being from New York, hadn't been driving for long and had already been in a couple of minor accidents. Rachel wanted to play her a tape of our album and couldn't work the car's tape player, so she took off her seat belt to lean over and figure it out. When Sheila looked down to try and help, she took her eyes off the road and ran the car into a guardrail on the winding part of Sunset Boulevard in the Pacific Palisades. Rachel smashed into the dashboard, splitting her head open from scalp to nose. The fact that she didn't have her seat belt on may have saved her life, though, because just as she fell across Sheila's lap, the entire passenger side of the car was completely smashed.

When I got the hysterical call from Sheila (as well as one from a nurse), I immediately rushed to the hospital.

All I knew was that Rachel had been badly hurt, but I didn't know any other details. I got Scotti to go with me, because I didn't think it would be right to take Joan. Anyway, Joan would have felt hypocritical going there and comforting Rachel while she was secretly with me.

When I got to St. John's Hospital in Santa Monica, I learned that Rachel's injuries weren't life threatening, but right away I saw that she was a mess—her whole head was bandaged, her face was swollen, her eyes were starting to blacken, and there was a lot of dried blood in her hair. It was far more than just a bad cut.

Later that night, when I went to check in on her, she grabbed my hand.

"How are you doing?" I asked as tenderly as I could.

"Did you call your mom?" she responded, her voice thick from pain medication.

"Yeah, don't worry about it," I told her. "A surgeon's on the way."

"Is he good?" she asked.

"Don't worry. He's supposed to be the best at facial reconstruction in all of L.A. He'll have you looking like your old self in no time."

"My career is over," Rachel said melodramatically. "Nobody wants to look at a rock star with a huge scar down the middle of her face."

"You're being ridiculous," I told her. "When the doctor's finished with you, no one will even notice it. Besides, no one can see anything under your bangs anyway." Luckily for Rachel, she'd been wearing her hair in severe Cleopatra-style bangs. She was obsessed with those bangs, making sure our hairdresser cut them perfectly straight.

I could tell she wasn't relieved by my mention of her bangs, but she changed the subject anyway. "While I was alone in the car, when Sheila went for help," she said, "I kept thinking about us."

I was totally uncomfortable with where this was headed.

"Please, let's give it another chance." She looked up at me with tears in her eyes.

"Don't even worry about that right now," I said sweetly, staying noncommittal. "All you have to concentrate on is getting through this."

"Please come back to the house," she begged. "Let's start over. Things can be different. This would never have happened if we were still together." She probably meant that if she hadn't been trying to spend the night with Sheila, she wouldn't have gotten into the accident— but I didn't know at the time that she had been planning to do that.

"This is a sign, Chas, that we're meant to be together."

I felt terrible for her, because she was so hurt and scared. Of course she would want me back with her at a time like this, but I didn't want to stay with her. A terrible pattern had developed, with Rachel going through these crises and then trying to pull me back.

"Don't worry, Rachel," I reassured her yet again, "I'll help you through this."

"That's not what I mean. Promise me you'll come back to the house."

I said nothing.

"Promise me," she repeated, this time more insistently.

Finally, reluctantly, I gave in. "I promise." Then a nurse came in to change Rachel's dressing, which had become almost completely soaked with blood. As I headed out of the room, I glanced back as the nurse took off the bandages. I was shocked to see Rachel's forehead—bone was showing through a gap of several inches, where the skin had rolled back to the side of her head. I thought I was going to either throw up or faint, or both.

I spent most of the night and morning at the hospital, waiting for the surgeon to arrive. The doctors kept the wound open until she could be sewn up. When the surgeon finally arrived, Rachel was awake for the procedure, but very doped up. It took him several hours to reconstruct her properly. She was pretty lucky, the doctors informed us, as she'd been just millimeters away from losing an eye.

Scotti stayed a few more hours with us, then left once everything had calmed down. Sheila went home too, and Amy and I ended up taking Rachel home in Amy's car. All the stitching had been done in the emergency room; the hospital never even admitted her.

I stayed with Rachel for a week while she recuperated, and her mom flew out right away to help. At first Rachel couldn't do anything for herself; her eyes were practically swollen shut and she was in a lot of pain. If this had happened when we were a tight couple, I would have felt incredibly empathetic and wanted to make everything better for her; I would have wanted to be her primary caregiver. But now I didn't feel that way at all. All I could think about the whole time I was with her was that I couldn't wait to leave and go back to Joan. As the week wore on and Rachel became less helpless, I resented having to be there at all.

After she felt well enough to travel, Rachel returned to New York with her mom to finish her recuperation. I went back to Joan's, where I now kept a bunch of my clothes. My comings and goings were becoming more difficult for Joan; she was frustrated that each time something happened to Rachel, I went off to be with her. Joan was starting to wonder whether she could depend on me and whether I was giving her top priority, especially because she was now giving me that priority. When she returned from Hawaii she had promptly broken up with Connie, and soon after that she ended her relationship with Leslie. (She did go out on a date with a guy, though, because I still wasn't physically available to her. Joan always wanted me to know that until I committed to a relationship with her, she'd keep her options open.)

Still, I was getting closer and closer to making a full commitment to Joan. While Rachel was back East, I decided to finally let my mom know about my relationship with Joan. I went to see her at her house and nervously tried to get out the words.

"There's something I need to tell you, Mom, but I don't know how you'll react, and it could really upset you..." I stumbled along. I feared she might be appalled simply because Joan was been a friend of hers. Considering my dramatic buildup, she braced herself for something horrible. So when I finally blurted, "I've been seeing Joan," she just laughed with relief. Then she said something really kind and understanding: "This will be a good life experience for you." My mom had always liked Joan and knew she was a good person who would treat me well—which is something she didn't think Rachel had always done. As for the age difference, my mom wasn't particularly concerned about that. She herself had often dated younger men, as had my grandmother, so age wasn't an issue.

✳

In September, Rachel returned to Los Angeles, healed enough to start working again. I was still traveling back and forth to Joan's. Then something happened that forced the issue for me.

Joan's cancer, up to that point, had been only a minor thought in the back of my mind. She'd been in remission for a year and a half. But one afternoon while I was at her house, she came back from a quarterly checkup with bad news: The cancer had returned. She was visibly upset and frightened. She'd been feeling so good that she'd expected a clean bill of health from her doctor, so the negative report completely shocked her. Now she'd have to go back on oral chemotherapy.

I had a strange reaction to the news. What I was going through with Rachel was so complicated and awful that the idea of losing someone to death, rather than in a messy breakup, seemed somehow nobler to me. I know that sounds terrible, but I was so young then. If Joan could live another five to ten years, that seemed like a good long time to me. I fantasized that we'd carry on a wonderful relationship during those years, that we'd never have to break up, and that if she died it would be peaceful. Dying, to me, didn't entail months of suffering, just a sudden ending. "Till death do us part"—isn't that a storybook image? In my distorted scenario, I wouldn't have to go through what I was going through with Rachel. I was incredibly naive and utterly insensitive on top of that.

I spent the rest of that day and evening with Joan, trying to be comforting. I reminded her that the oral chemo had worked well the last time and only had a few side effects. I tried to convince her that it would put her back into remission and that she'd soon be fine again.

Joan and I made love that evening and into the night. For me, making love to her was the ultimate caregiving, the best way to take her mind off the cancer. I believed sex could fix everything. Afterward, as we lay in bed, I held her and we talked. At one point she became really upset and started crying. I tried to soothe her, but suddenly I remembered I'd told Rachel I'd spend the night at *her* place. This was nothing out of the ordinary—I was constantly going back and forth, and I had told Joan I'd be going there before she had gone to her doctor's appointment. She was fine with that, but of course neither of us had expected her to come back with bad news. Nonetheless, I started to obsess about returning to Rachel's, afraid that if I didn't, something horrible would happen. It was an irrational fear, like the one I'd felt as a kid when I'd broken the glass in the hotel room.

There wasn't any special reason for me to be at Rachel's that night—I was just trying to placate her. Maybe I'd spent a couple of nights at Joan's that week, so I was trying to balance it out by telling Rachel I'd be home that night. I didn't want to not come home and risk her getting pissed off at me.

I'd been seeing a therapist since the beginning of the summer, trying to gain the courage to break it off completely with Rachel. It had been my own idea to go, and I'd found the therapist on the recommendation of one of my doctors. The therapist would try to confront my irrational fears by talking me through a worst-case scenario. In this particular case, it would be something like, "If you don't go back to Rachel's, what's the worst that could happen?" My response would be, "She'll get mad at me." Then the therapist would say, "What else would she do to you?" And I'd respond, "Well, nothing. She'll just get mad!" And the therapist would ask, "How bad could that be?" But having someone be angry at me was bad enough—it terrified me. I guess that's why Joan somehow got the short end of the stick. Joan didn't get mad at me, while Rachel did, and my decisions were too often based on who would get the least angry.

That's why I made the ridiculous decision to leave Joan that night, even though I knew it was absolutely wrong. I knew that the right thing was to stay and be there for her in the morning. But no, I left in the middle of the night, driven away by my anxiety over Rachel's possible displeasure. I felt like I'd just fucked and ran. If Joan was upset about my leaving, she hid it from me.

And then, wouldn't you know it, Rachel didn't even come home that night. This turn of events kept me from sleeping, as I dwelled on how awful my behavior had been. I'd been unfair to Rachel because of my fear of her, I'd been unfair to Joan, and I'd been unfair to myself. I was shocked that I'd left Joan that night; I couldn't believe I could do something so insensitive and heartless. After a night of soul searching, I came to the conclusion that I should have reached long before: I had to break up with Rachel now and for good. The only way to guarantee that she'd take me seriously this time was to finally admit that I'd been with Joan and wanted to stay with her. The reality of Joan's condition hit me in a different way that night: I'd fallen in love with a woman with cancer who was sick again, yet I was taking my time making a commitment to her because I was too scared and weak to stand up to Rachel. I finally understood that I didn't know how much longer Joan would be around and I didn't have any more time to waste.

When Rachel returned at seven A.M., I was sitting up in bed, wide awake. She didn't seem to feel guilty about having been out all night—it wasn't as if we'd made special plans for the evening.

"Hi, what are you doing up?" she asked as she came into the bedroom. I rarely got up before nine A.M.

"I've been up all night," I said testily. "Didn't I tell you I'd spend the night here?"

"Yeah?"

"So where were you last night?"

"You told me *you* were spending the night here last night—I never told you I was going to."

"Well, I guess I just figured you'd be here."

"Just because you were going to grace me with your presence, you figured I'd drop everything?" Rachel said, anger rising in her voice. She'd been changing her clothes, but then she stopped and faced me. "First you tell me you aren't sure you want to be with me anymore and that you need space, even though we'd just started recording the record we spent four years busting our asses to make. Then, after you take a break, you come home and say you want to work on our relationship. Then you come up with the brilliant idea that the best way to work on our relationship is to make it an open one. And then you think you want to break up with me again, so you encourage me to start dating other people. So *that's* where I was last night: on a date. Do you have a problem with that? Maybe you'd like to change your mind again."

"No," I said quietly.

"You've become so fucking wishy-washy, it makes me sick," Rachel continued.

"It makes me sick too," I said. "Speaking of sick, Joan's cancer is back."

"Is that why you were up all night?" Rachel asked, calming down.

"That's part of the reason."

Rachel sat on the edge of the bed. "Will you finally just be honest with me?" she said, suddenly calm and rational. "The hardest part of this whole thing has been the lying. I know you've been sleeping with her, and yet you keep denying it. It makes me feel like I'm going crazy." She paused for a moment and looked me dead in the eyes. "Chas, please tell me the truth. Please, finally admit that you're having a relationship with Joan."

"Yes," I said.

Rachel looked confused for a second. Perhaps she hadn't really expected me to admit anything. "Yes that you'll tell me the truth, or yes that you've been having an affair with Joan?"

"Yes, I've been having a relationship with Joan. I've fallen in love with her. And I want to be with her." I paused. "It's really over between you and me, Rachel. I promise I won't change my mind again."

Rachel didn't get angry, but at this point it didn't matter how she reacted. It was really over. When I was scared and sheepish and didn't know how to extricate myself from the relationship, her anger would have intimidated me. Now it wouldn't change anything. I'd suddenly reached utter clarity and honesty. I was sick of the game I'd been playing, and my priorities had fallen firmly into place. I wanted to be with Joan a hundred percent so that we could spend whatever time she had left together.

✳

Soon after that night, Rachel went to New York to be with her family. I started looking for an apartment but couldn't find anything I liked. I would have loved to have moved in with Joan, but I didn't want to be presumptuous, and she hadn't asked. Still, I spent most of my time there. My mom finally said, "Why don't you just keep your stuff at my house, instead of spending money on a place of your own?" I thought that was a good idea, but somehow my stuff never got to my mom's; it found its way to Joan's instead.

I was worried what Scotti would think of me living with Joan, but she was all right with it. She knew Joan wasn't happy with the other women she'd been seeing, and Scotti had been annoyed by all the drama in those relationships. In comparison, my relationship with Joan—when other people weren't in our way—was almost drama-free. Besides, Scotti had known me forever and liked me. Her positive feelings for both Joan and me outweighed the strangeness of the situation for Scotti, just as they had for my mom.

In New York, Rachel became very depressed over our breakup and started to see a therapist. She was so down, in fact, that the therapist sent her to a psychiatrist who prescribed Prozac for her. Rachel needed to get herself together and return to Los Angeles so we could form our band, but she had a very bad reaction to the Prozac: It sent her into a manic episode, during which she couldn't sleep at all. Rachel had always been drug sensitive—one of those people who can barely take an antihistamine— and knew something was wrong, but her family thought she was just anxious about returning to Los Angeles. Her mother flew back to L.A. with her to help her get settled, but when they arrived Amy noticed that Rachel's pupils were quite dilated. Rachel was also having auditory and visual hallucinations, as if she were on acid. She was drinking alcohol to try to stop the hallucinations, but it didn't help at all.

Like Amy, I spotted Rachel's dilated pupils right away when I came to visit, so I called my mom to have her help us find a good psychiatrist or psychopharmacologist. My mom has always had excellent doctors, and through them we can always find others who are tops in their fields. She eventually found a psychopharmacologist for Rachel who told her that the Prozac had caused the manic episode. It wasn't enough for her to just stop taking it, he explained, as the Prozac could stay in her system for another two to six weeks. So the doctor prescribed a heavy-duty tran- quilizer to counteract the manic episodes and allow Rachel to sleep and function.

I felt sorry for Rachel and a bit guilty, because I knew our breakup had caused her to take the antidepressants. I was also concerned about how her illness would affect our work schedule. Bottom line, I still loved Rachel and was concerned about her as a friend—that's why I'd called my mom—but I didn't want to get pulled back in by her.

Nonetheless, Joan still felt suspicious about any atten- tion I showed her. When I returned from visiting Rachel, Joan acted rather distant.

"Hi, baby," I said, finding her in the kitchen washing dishes. She kept her hands in the sink when I leaned in to hug and kiss her.

"What a scene it is over there," I said, sitting on the kitchen countertop and reaching out to massage Joan's shoulder. "Rachel is completely bugged out, and she's got her mom and Amy and Donna all trying to figure out what to do for her."

"Rachel is always bugging out," said Joan, her eyes still focused on the dishes. "She's probably just trying to manipulate you into moving back."

"No, baby, I think this is for real. I even got the name of a shrink for her."

"How long are you going to continue to bail her out?" asked Joan, resentment apparent in her voice. "Are you always going to clean up her messes?"

I was a little taken aback, and a little pissed off. Joan had had the same sort of push-me, pull-you relationship with Leslie, so it was sort of like the pot calling the kettle black.

Taking my hand from her shoulder, I said, "Besides the fact that Rachel's been in my life for almost five years, she's still my business partner. This could potentially fuck up our release date."

"That's always your excuse—that it'll fuck up your record. If it hasn't been fucked up by now, with everything that's happened, it's not going to get fucked up."

I didn't say anything; I just stood there reflecting on whether Joan was right. She finished the dishes, turned off the faucet, wiped her hands on a dishtowel, and turned to me. Her eyes looked watery. "So when are you leaving?" she asked.

I look at her, puzzled. "What do you mean?"

"I mean, when are you leaving to move back in with Rachel and take care of her again?"

Finally I realized why she'd been acting in a way that seemed insensitive. The expression on my face turned to compassion. "I'm not leaving," I tried to reassure her.

"Why not? You always have in the past."

I got off the counter and took a step forward, taking Joan's hand. "I told you that this time will be different, and I meant it."

"Why? Why is this any different?"

"Because I finally told her the truth about us, Joan. I told her that she and I are really over." I hugged Joan and she hugged me back. Then I said softly in her ear, "Don't you get it, baby? I want to spend the rest of my life with you. Till death do us part."

✳

Unfortunately, Rachel reacted just as poorly to the tranquilizer as she had to the Prozac. After taking the first dose in the car on the way home from the pharmacy, she didn't remember much else for weeks. The drug affected her short-term memory so severely that she could barely carry on a conversation. In fact, we couldn't work with her in this condition. One day we tried to do an interview with a Geffen publicist for our press kit, but Rachel couldn't provide much coherent information. When she later read a copy of the bio the publicist wrote from the interview, she was blown away that we had even let her do the interview in the state she was in.

Rachel's family took her back to New York once again

and checked her into Sloan Kettering's psychiatric department for a few weeks. While there she called her New York therapist, who told her to stop taking the tranquilizers. So she hid them under her tongue and finally started to get better.

In comparison to Rachel, Joan and I were doing great. She could finally stop worrying that I was going to go back to Rachel, and I could focus all my attention on her. But I also had to keep working on forming a band, even though Rachel was in New York. We were under a great deal of pressure from the record company, so Rich and I decided to conduct auditions without her.

With Rachel not around, wouldn't you know it, Rich started hitting on *me,* but I quickly shut him down: "Rich, come on! Give me a break. You're going to do this because Rachel's not here? Forget about it!" Despite his unwanted attention, it was otherwise nice to be working with him. Without Rachel around, my opinion was finally beginning to count. I have to admit that part of me wished Rachel would stay in New York, because the drama in my life had vanished and I was being taken seriously as an artist.

The record company, by this time, was pretty annoyed with Rachel. She was now in a mental institution, after all, and had previously held up our work with her various accidents. There was some talk of firing her, but when push came to shove I stood up for her. I went to a meeting with John Kalodner and told him that if Rachel could get herself together and still wanted to be part of the band, then I wanted her to do it. I did it out of loyalty. I knew it would make my life a hundred times easier to do it without her, but she had worked just as hard for this as I had—perhaps even harder. It meant the world to her. We were so close to achieving our dream, and I couldn't let the record company fire her for the sake of my own comfort.

Meanwhile, Rich and I finished choosing a band, mostly married guys in their thirties, and started to put together a live show. But we still didn't have a band name. We wanted to call ourselves Pandora's Box, but a European band had already taken that name. We even tried to buy the rights from them but couldn't.

It's ironic—or maybe fitting—that we desperately wanted a name that *Webster's* defines as "a prolific source of troubles."

※

By the time Rachel flew back to Los Angeles, around Halloween, I was happily living with Joan. During the time she'd been away, Joan and I had told everyone who hadn't known before that we were lovers. We no longer had to hide.

For Joan and me, Halloween was the best night of the year. Joan had always loved the holiday because she enjoyed dressing up flamboyantly. For me, it was the one night when I could comfortably go out to gay bars, concealed by a costume and thus unrecognizable. This year I dressed up as Zorro, complete with a fencing saber and paste-on mustache, while Joan was Lady Godiva, wearing a nude-colored leotard and a down-to-her-knees blond wig.

We spent the night with a group of friends, chauffeured around in a limousine. First we stopped at a party given by a woman named Laura (who would become my lover some years later). Then we headed to the legendary lesbian bar The Palms, an old dive that seemed to be the place to gather that night. We had a good time just drinking and dancing and being openly affectionate with each other. It was unbelievable that Joan and I could finally dance together and not have to pretend we weren't lovers.

I finally felt free. All my friends whom I'd worried would find out about Joan and me had proven to be wonderfully supportive. They'd known Joan since I'd moved back to Los Angeles and knew what a sweet and giving person she was. There was nothing *not* to like about Joan—her door was always open, and she went out of her way to take care of people. Besides, they could see how happy I was with her. And it had been quite a while since my friends had seen me happy.

Since she was such a festive person, Joan always made a big deal out of the winter holiday season. She usually hosted a huge Thanksgiving feast to feed all her friends (and any strays they'd bring along), but this year we were invited to Joshua Tree, a stunning desert area about two hours outside of Los Angeles. A friend of hers had a cabin there and asked about eight others to come celebrate.

I was by far the youngest, so it was a little strange for me. I could tell there was a bit of envy over Joan having such a young girlfriend, but instead of giving her a hard time, they congratulated her, saying things like, "You go, girl!" They made me feel like I was a prize of some sort, which was weird. Although they were in their forties and quite grown up in comparison to me, these women seemed, in retrospect, rather immature. They were not unlike Joan in that most of them weren't career-driven, and several were "kept" in some degree by husbands or boyfriends while maintaining female lovers on the side. They also had a lot of drama in their relationships, many of which were of the old-school butch-femme variety. My peers weren't into such role-playing.

When it was just Joan and me together, I didn't notice how different our worlds were. At Joshua Tree, the best solution was for us to go off by ourselves, taking drives through the gorgeous desert landscape and stopping for picnics. The Thanksgiving dinner itself turned out to be delicious, thanks to the fact that Joan cooked it.

I was more comfortable around Joan's friends when Joan and I were the ones doing the entertaining. Now that we were together, we hosted a lot of dinner parties at the Hooky House. Joan always made sure we had our friends' favorite foods and drinks on hand, and we spent hours trying out new recipes and creating elaborate meals. Joan excelled at spaghetti sauce, and I specialized in barbecuing breaded Sicilian steaks, but we were willing to try anything. At one party, for example, we made hors d'oeuvres from around the world, including sushi, Russian potato slices with caviar, and Chinese dumplings.

Compared to my friends and me, Joan was quite sophisticated. At the house I'd shared with Rachel and Amy, all the furniture was from IKEA, except for the bedroom set my mother had bought me. But Joan had "real" furniture, and when she cooked a meal, it featured all the proper courses: cocktails, appetizers, main dish, wine, and dessert. The plates and silverware all matched, and we used place mats.

Between Thanksgiving and New Year's, the record business shut down, so Joan and I spent lazy days together, going to matinees or packing a picnic lunch and venturing off somewhere. Sometimes we had picnics in our own backyard.

Joan was masterful at keeping romance alive. She didn't want us to become too comfortable as a couple, so she always tried to make our times together special, dressing up for me and insisting we go out for romantic dinners or enjoy candlelit meals at home.

She also liked to keep some mystery and manners about her. Let's just say she was the kind of person who insisted on closing the bathroom door. As for our sex life, it took me a while to get used to how often she wanted to make love. While I had been involved in a way-too-comfortable relationship with Rachel (in other words, there wasn't much sex in our later years together), Joan was dating various women and had become used to having sex every time she got together with someone. When I moved in with her, we were having sex perhaps three times a week, which to me seemed like a lot. Imagine my surprise, then, when she said to me one day, "Chas, this isn't working for me. We've got to step it up here." Three times a week wasn't enough for her! Of course I didn't want her to be dissatisfied, and it wasn't a chore to meet her need for more sex. I respected Joan's views about sex and romance because too many lesbian relationships become so close and cozy that sensuality and romance often fall by the wayside. Joan had seen that happen to others and was determined not to let it happen to her.

For Christmas I decided to go to my family gathering in Aspen without Joan. I felt that my family's knowledge of our relationship was too fresh and perhaps a bit controversial. Joan understood, though we both knew we'd miss each other.

But we had a great Christmastime together before I headed for the mountains. Joan went all out to decorate the house: Poinsettias lined the walkway, a big wreath hung on the door, and on the wall around her wet bar she'd woven a garland of pine branches, pine cones, and oranges spiced with cloves and cinnamon sticks. It smelled wonderful. Below the bar she displayed an old-fashioned, Norman Rockwell-ish, Christmas USA snow town that lit up. She chose a Hawaiian theme for the Christmas tree (theme trees were her annual tradition), decorating it in Hawaii's state colors, red and gold. Outside the house she created a California snowman out of tumbleweeds she'd spray-painted white.

We burned cozy fires in the fireplace and served gallons of egg nog and spiced cider with brandy to friends who dropped by. This gracious life wasn't what Joan had grown up with. I think she had the opposite sort of experience in her home, where her stepfather beat her and her mother felt jealous of her beauty and didn't protect her. So Joan had compensated by becoming the perfect hostess, especially at holidays. She created a setting pleasing to almost all the senses: beautiful to look at, wonderful to smell, luscious to taste, and filled with perfect holiday music.

The morning before I went to Aspen, Joan and I pretended it was our own Christmas Day and opened the gifts we'd gotten each other. As usual, Joan was very generous, giving me numerous presents, my favorite being a Harley Davidson leather motorcycle jacket. She also gave me two classic men's bags stocked with toiletries and a nail clipper set. Back then I had simply used zip-lock bags for my toiletries. Joan was so thoughtful about so many things.

My gift to her wasn't particularly romantic, but in a way it showed her how precious she was to me: a Derringer gun with a mother-of-pearl handle, small enough for her to carry in her purse. Such a seemingly odd present makes sense only if you realize that growing up in a famous family made me feel vulnerable and unsafe. My mom received death threats all the time, and a security guard stayed at our house every night. My family legally owned guns and so did I (as did Joan). Even though it was a misdemeanor to carry a concealed weapon in California, I wanted Joan to have one to give us both a sense of security, especially at a time when carjacking had become headline news in L.A. It's not something I'd do today, but then it seemed appropriate.

We spent the rest of that day marveling at our good fortune. Both of us believed in destiny: We knew we were meant to be together, but we didn't take it for granted, feeling so much gratitude for what we had finally achieved. That night, Joan and I made love on a faux fur blanket in front of the fireplace. *It doesn't get much better than this,* I thought.

The next day I took off for Aspen. In the five days I was away, Joan continued to take her oral chemo treatments, which she'd begun in October. Fortunately, other than leaving her with less energy than usual, the chemo didn't have any terrible side effects. We'd both assumed it would be successful, because it had worked twice before. Her doctor didn't think there was any reason to assume otherwise. In fact, the treatment regimen was more of an inconvenience than a cause for concern.

*

After a quiet New Year's back at home with Joan, my musical life picked up steam again, as we prepared for a spring release of the album. Rachel and I were still solidifying the band, replacing our bass player after he got another gig and rehearsing our live show at a studio in West Los Angeles where Rich knew the owners. Yes, Rich was guiding our rehearsals, but things had calmed down among the three of us. Rachel and I were getting along pretty well too, though she still harbored a lot of anger toward Joan. Even though Rachel had a new girlfriend of her own, who came to our rehearsals all the time, she didn't want Joan to be there.

"If you bring Joan to a rehearsal, I'm walking out," she told me. Stupidly, I let her have her way—and paid the emotional price with Joan, who thought it was unfair. In New York, our friends had always come to rehearsals, and now everyone was allowed to drop in except the most important person in my life. Joan was pissed off at me for not standing up to Rachel, and she was right: There was no way Rachel would have walked out of a rehearsal. But I still believed some of Rachel's threats.

Our past relationships were just about the only things Joan and I argued about. She got frustrated about Rachel, and I got pissed off at the lack of boundaries she had with Leslie. Neither of us had done a great job of totally separating from our past lives and loves. But Joan would go out dancing with Les (with whom she'd remained friends) only to make a point with me: She was frustrated that I wouldn't go with her to bars because I was still closeted. I certainly wanted to go—and it drove me crazy that she was dancing with Leslie instead of me—but I felt I couldn't. Joan told me I was being ridiculous. She kept making the point that k.d. lang and Melissa Etheridge had come out of the closet and it hadn't negatively affected their careers, so why was I worried?

At the beginning of that year, 1993, Rachel and I decided to formally address the issue of our sexual orientation with Geffen Records. We had a big meeting at their offices with David Geffen himself, publicity head Brynn Bridenthal, company head Eddie Rosenblatt, and John Kalodner. My mom even showed up.

We met in a large conference room in the windowless basement, sitting around a long, gorgeous wood table in handsome leather chairs. We wished we didn't have to deal with this situation—it wasn't like we were getting together to discuss something fun like making a video or finding out how much everyone liked the album—but it was necessary. Whenever I had thought about doing press, I was terrified, because I knew this issue would come up.

Brynn, a very smart, forty-something woman who looked both stylish and intellectual, did most of the talking for the company. We had met with her before, in preparation for our upcoming press tour, and she taught us a lot about feeling comfortable with reporters and not letting them bully us. She stressed that we had to communicate what *we* wanted a reporter to know, no matter what questions were asked. She talked about how we should focus on our music, rather than the gossipy stuff about my family or our sexual orientation. I think she was also the person who told us not to get overly concerned about any article once it came out, because whatever's on the newsstand today wraps fish tomorrow.

The gist of the hour-long meeting was that Geffen Records wanted us to know that we were under no pressure to deny our sexual orientation. Brynn had been going through this stuff with David Geffen for a long time and had dealt with both his dodging the issue of his sexuality and then being honest about it. With David out of the closet, it would have been hypocritical for them to say we couldn't be as well.

"We'll handle the press any way you want to deal with it," Brynn told us. Then we all the discussed the pros and cons of staying in the closet. My mom actually encouraged us to come out.

"There's a lot of honesty and integrity in your music, so how can you convincingly sell your music and hide this?" my mom asked us. "How can you be truthful in your music while lying about who you are?" That's my mom for you: always unflinchingly honest.

John Kalodner, on the other hand, was surprisingly conservative. "I'm concerned that you'll limit your audience," he said. "Sex plays a big part in the music industry, and you don't want to turn off a male audience that might be attracted to you." I guess he didn't subscribe to the notion that a lot of young rock 'n' roll guys might be *drawn* to two young, attractive lesbians.

Rachel and I were torn. At the time of my tabloid outing, no musician had come out except Elton John, who'd said in *Rolling Stone* that he was bisexual. After that, his career took a nosedive. But with k.d. and Melissa not suffering any decline in popularity from being out (which certainly made our record company more comfortable about us being out), things had changed. Nonetheless, Rachel and I were still reeling from the tabloid experience.

Everyone's reaction had been so negative at that time that we felt, in a sense, brainwashed.

So our response at that meeting was that we were afraid to come out definitively. We were afraid that it would narrow the scope of our audience. Even though it hadn't affected Melissa and k.d., we figured they'd already had established careers when they came out. Rachel and I were still unknowns. Would people accept us being gay before they had a chance to hear our music? I was scared to find out.

"We don't feel comfortable lying about it," I said. "But is there a way that we could not admit it and not deny it either? You know, do a tap dance around it?"

"That's fine, if it's your decision," said Brynn. "We just want you to know that we're behind you, whatever you choose to do."

In the weeks after the meeting, Rachel and I met with Brynn to hammer out a strategy. We finally decided this: If asked, we wouldn't deny being lesbians, but we wouldn't confirm it either. (In later years I laughed when I saw other public figures do the same thing. As if the rest of us didn't know the truth!) Basically, we developed a few stock answers if asked about our sexuality. My answer would be that I didn't want to limit myself to a potential partner based on anything—race, religion, nationality, or, oh yes, gender. And that was all true—except for the gender part. I was so rock 'n' roll and open-minded and cool. Rachel would say something to the effect that rock 'n' roll has always been about sex and sexuality, and she didn't want to ruin anybody's fantasy about her by saying anything one way or another. "Whatever turns them on is how they should think of me," she'd say.

The fact that we had broken up made things easier. When people asked us, "Are you two lovers?" we could convincingly say, "No." I guess they should have asked, "Are you now or have you ever been..." But they didn't.

With that solved, at least for the moment, we finally chose a name for our band: Ceremony. Rachel came up with it, because as a Deadhead she considered concerts to be ceremonial. I loved the name. Having been to eight zillion Dead concerts with Rachel, I liked the ceremonial aspect even more than the music. Dead shows are events, period, not just musical events. I wanted our music and live shows to be about more than just music— I wanted them to evoke feelings about life and love. A song can take you back, help you through a hard time, give voice to exactly what you're going through.

Even though Rachel had come up with the name, she wasn't nearly as sold on it as I was, nor was Rich. But all the other names we put on the table were already taken by other bands. Ceremony was free and clear, and that's what ultimately made our decision.

Work now became exciting for us. We were pleased with the guys in the band, and we were doing a lot of press, tons of photo shoots, and a steady round of rehearsals. We even shot a video for the song that would be our first single, "Could Have Been Love." The settings included the landmark Crossroads of the World, a 1936 Hollywood architectural hodgepodge that was the world's first modern shopping mall and is now an office complex. The Crossroads shoot was done at night, and all our friends—Donna, Amy, Scotti, and others—served as extras, dressed up like Rachel and me in hippie garb. While the band played, our friends danced around us as if they were at a party. Even Joan showed up in costume and ready to dance, as Rachel had finally stopped being completely resistant to her presence. The two of them weren't buddy-buddy, but Rachel was solid in another relationship by this time and knew it would have been unfair not to allow Joan to be in our video.

✳

Although our schedule was busy, I had weekends off, so Joan and I spent them relaxing or taking short getaways. For Valentine's Day we headed to San Diego, arriving late in the afternoon and spending a romantic night in the hotel room. We ordered room service and champagne and exchanged presents.

I opened my package first: a pair of beautiful black silk pajamas.

"Thank you, baby," I threw my arms around her. "Now open yours!" I couldn't wait for her to see what I'd gotten her.

Joan opened the small, gold package, which was wrapped with a ribbon and a bow. Inside was a black velvet box, and inside that a narrow gold band featuring an amethyst stone cut into a heart shape, with tiny diamonds set on each side. I'd bought it from one of her favorite jewelers in Beverly Hills, Pepe. Joan stared at it for a moment, then looked at me and smiled.

"I love it," she said.

"You sure? You looked at it for a while before you said anything."

"I'm sure. But I have to confess something: Ever since

I saw your gift box I've been worried what would happen if I didn't like it."

"Oh, you didn't have faith in my shopping expertise?" I grinned.

"Well, you've never bought me jewelry before, and that's such a personal thing." Joan took my hand, opened my palm, and put the ring in it, then held her left hand in front of me. "I love it," she said. "And I love you."

"I love you too." I slipped the ring on her finger, then leaned in to kiss her.

On another free weekend, we headed out to Palm Springs, staying in a charming hotel of bungalows furnished with a French country feel. Since we spent time lying by the pool, I made sure to put on sunscreen, because I'm pretty fair and hadn't developed my base tan for the year. At some point, though, I was lying with my arms behind my head—and I ended up burning my armpits, the one area I hadn't protected!

On one of our days in Palm Springs, we went to a water park, which turned out to be a blast. We slid down almost every slide, with Joan screaming like crazy. Everyone below her looked up to see who was making all the noise. I tried to pretend I didn't know her.

All day long I eyed the biggest slide with fear and desire. It was extremely steep—straight down for what seemed like a half-dozen stories. Joan said there was no way she'd go on it. Finally, at the end of the day, I got up the courage to try it myself. I was like a young guy trying to impress my girl; I wanted to show her how virile and fearless I was. Silly me—the ride was terrifying. You slide down on your back, but it's so steep that you feel like you're going to fall forward. As you hit the straightaway at the end, you whack back and forth against the sides, acting as your own set of brakes. Then, when you hit the water, you get a liquid injection up every orifice of your body. It's really unpleasant. I've since been back to that park with my younger brother and sister, but I'll never go down that slide again. So much for my macho side.

✳

At the end of March, just before the band was scheduled for a short tour, Joan and I went back to Hawaii. We were alone there, for a change, and had a fabulous time. We boogie-boarded at our favorite beaches, ate at our favorite restaurants, and soaked up all the pleasures of paradise. At a luau we attended, we asked a friend of Joan's to take a couple of pictures with our camera. We didn't have any pictures of us before that, because I was still so paranoid of there being "proof" that I was gay. Because of our age difference, I was even more paranoid of someone getting hold of pictures of me with Joan. I had no idea what people would make of that—not only is Chastity Bono a lesbian, but she's going out with someone her mom's age! I was hesitant having those pictures taken in Hawaii, but I'm now so happy that I have them to remember our time together in the place we both loved.

In April, the Ceremony tour began. First we played a few gigs around Southern California that were within driving distance, one of them being in Palm Springs. I drove there with Joan and met up with a number of our L.A. friends who drove there separately. We stayed with

Jeannie, the woman who had been with us in Hawaii, and our friends took motel rooms.

The audience at our show included my family too: my dad, who was the mayor of Palm Springs at the time; his wife Mary; and my half-sister Christy, who's ten years older than me. Joan and I had spent a lot of time with Christy at the restaurant she owned on Main Street in Santa Monica—Bono Fortuna—and Christy and Joan got along wonderfully.

The next day most of the band returned to L.A., but Joan and I planned to spend the day with our friends hanging out at Jeannie's condo pool. She was worried, however, that we'd cause a ruckus and get her in trouble, so I asked my dad if we could hang out at his pool. I slightly downplayed the number of people I was bringing—he probably didn't expect six of us to show up and take over—but we ended up having a really nice time. It was the first chance Dad and Joan had gotten to talk and spend time together, and they ended up feeling quite comfortable with each other. I was really glad he liked her. It wasn't critical for me to have my parents bless my choice of girlfriend, but it certainly felt good.

After Joan and I returned to Los Angeles, I came down with a bad flu, so our band had to cancel a couple of gigs that were scheduled. By now the band had rented a tour van, which they drove to Texas, where we were booked at a Hard Rock Cafe. I flew to meet them for the show, which turned out to be a disaster. The power cut out several times during our set, until the club realized they didn't have enough power to handle both our sound system and lighting rig. We ended up finishing the performance with the house lights on! It probably would have been better to play in the dark instead, because you don't want to see people eating while you're performing on stage.

I then drove with the band to New Orleans, still feeling pretty sick and suffering from insomnia because of the antihistamine I was taking. Fortunately, our tour ended on a much better note there, at Geffen Records' annual convention for its promotion people. We opened for another Geffen act, and our set went well, stirring a positive buzz about us.

Being in New Orleans was otherwise uncomfortable, as Geffen Records put us up in a fleabag motel with ripped wallpaper and stains on the carpet. *Entertainment Tonight* was doing a story on us, following us around to our gig and to the French Market in the French Quarter. (They wanted silly footage of us trying on masks and headdresses, supposedly showing us in our "everyday life.") People who later watched the piece probably thought we were kidding when we delivered a sarcastic tour of our crummy motel rooms. Or maybe they thought it had been staged to show that we weren't on a star trip. But I would have loved to stay at a classier place, especially since I was still fighting the flu.

On top of being sick, most of my professional responsibilities on the tour felt embarrassing. I felt stupid in my rock 'n' roll clothes, and I hated doing staged events like the trip to the French Market. In fact, everything about the band seemed staged. We no longer had an organically formed group like we'd had in New York; we had hired guns who wouldn't have been playing with us if we weren't paying them. In New York, playing music with our friends had been more real, more fun, and felt much less stressful.

Now we were supposed to be demonstrating our "star quality," but I didn't feel like a star. I didn't have the attitude; I felt too insecure. I didn't think Rachel had it either, though she was more confident than I in certain areas and enjoyed the entire process more. Then again, she suffered from terrible stage fright. I felt like an impostor and she had stage fright—what was wrong with this picture?

I wasn't crazy about being on stage myself. Since our record hadn't come out and we didn't have a following yet, the only people who came to see us perform were either curious about me because of my parents or just happened to be at the venue where we were booked. Onstage I felt judged and I wasn't convinced I could win over an audience. I even felt judged by my bandmates, who looked at Rachel and me with some suspicion. One of them even asked us, point blank, "Come on, you didn't write any of these songs, did you?" It was hard to feel legitimate with so much incredulousness around us.

We were a little too nice to be rock stars. If Slash from Guns n' Roses walked into his A&R person's office and pissed on the desk, it would be spoken of admiringly— "That's rock 'n' roll!" The more guys acted out, the more record companies liked it. But Rachel and I didn't fit that lifestyle at all. We were trying to be so good. Ironically, the one thing that was slightly edgy and controversial about us was our sexual orientation, and that's the one thing we'd decided to hide. That would have at least made for an interesting story and gotten us a core audience.

On top of everything else, I was shocked by how much the press hounded me about my parents. I guess I shouldn't have been, but I was naive. "What do your parents think of your record? How much did they help you get your record deal? Did they sing backup on your record? How much of an influence is their music on you? What's it like to have Cher as a mom?" I was barraged by ridiculous questions that didn't have anything to do with what Rachel and I were trying to do musically. I was still just seen as the daughter of Sonny and Cher.

✳

In England, where we flew to in June for a ten-day tour, the press was a hundred times worse. The legitimate newspapers in London are more like America's tabloids, and their tabloids are nothing like those in the States. They're downright nasty. The questions veered so far off course I could scarcely believe them: "What do you and your mother like to do together? Where do you like to go shopping?" A journalist might act nice and polite at first, then ask, "What brand of tampon does your mother prefer?" Well, no one went quite that far, but they came pretty close: I was asked what kind of shoes my mom liked to wear. I finally lost my cool. "What do my mother's shoes have to do with my record?" I nearly screamed. I didn't want to be disrespectful, but sometimes I wanted to tell them to go fuck themselves.

The questions about my sexual orientation were particularly rude and intrusive. I kept giving them my stock answer: "As a musician I try to be very open-minded. For me, it's about the person. I try not to limit myself by race or gender or religion." That's not what I really felt about gender, of course; it was just my calculated evasion.

Other aspects of our English tour were a marked improvement, however. We made successful appearances on a morning TV show and at a club gig for record sellers and radio station people. Our record was released in England while we were there, and it was a thrill to walk into Tower Records and see our CD and single in the racks. We were also treated a lot better there by the record company (Warner Brothers, the parent company of Geffen) than we had been by Geffen Records in New Orleans. Rachel and I were given beautiful rooms at a lovely hotel, we were taken out for nice dinners, and the record company personnel genuinely seemed to like our music and wanted to create a pleasant experience for us.

Despite the difficulties making our record, I had remained optimistic about our music career. But in London I started to feel anxious; things didn't feel right. I wasn't sure if it would be worse to be a failure or a success. I hated being away from Joan, even on this short tour, so the idea of taking to the road for months at a time seemed horrifying. Rachel and I had started this project as a couple, so I never imagined that my lover wouldn't be with me while I was on tour.

Then again, if our record wasn't a hit, what was I going to do with my life? Damned if I do, damned if I don't. To my distress, I realized I'd picked a career I didn't really like. I'd latched onto a dream that really wasn't my dream. I didn't know what my dreams were, but I didn't feel qualified to do anything else.

I wanted to talk to Joan about all of this, but in England I couldn't afford long phone conversations since the rates were so high. Joan and I faxed letters to each other instead, and in her first faxes she sounded very sweet: "I miss you...can't wait until you get home..." But after about ten days, she seemed more distant. "I guess I'm getting used to you being away," she wrote. In fact, Joan wasn't used to being alone at all. She hadn't been in a monogamous relationship in years, and at least one of the women she dated was always around. Since she didn't work, her attention tended to focus on the person she was going out with. She wasn't very independent, which suited me fine for the most part because I wasn't either. But when she pulled back a little, I panicked.

Thinking about Joan's message, I couldn't sleep, so I decided to call her. It was two or three in the morning London time—six P.M. in L.A.—when Joan answered.

"Hi, baby. What are you doing?" I asked. I was excited just to reach her, because it was hard to coordinate our schedules because of the time difference.

"I'm straightening up the house," she answered. "Judy's coming over later, and I'm cooking for her." Judy was an old friend of hers.

"Oh, that sounds like fun—tell her I say hi. Honey, I'm going to be home in two days—I can't wait to see you!"

"Yeah, two more days," Joan said, as if that were a long time rather than soon.

"Honey, is everything OK there?"

"Yeah, it's fine," she said, trying to sound nonchalant.

"Well, aren't you excited to see me? I'm counting the minutes."

"I guess I'm excited."

"You *guess*?"

"Yeah."

"Joan, what's going on with you? Is something wrong?"

"Not really. You've just been away for so long that I've gotten used to it."

"What do you mean?"

"The first week that you were gone, I missed you so much and was feeling so lonely that it was driving me crazy. So I guess I've started to detach a little bit, rather than be miserable without you. I think it's a defense mechanism."

I didn't like that reaction at all. I hadn't shut down— I'd missed her the entire time I'd been away. I didn't have *any* defense mechanisms, damn it!

"Joan," I said, getting annoyed, "I've only been gone ten days! What are you going to do when I go on the road for a couple of months?"

"Well, that's just it. I guess I'm practicing for when that happens."

"But you're making me feel like shit! Here I am, going out of my mind, counting the seconds until I see you, and you're making me feel like you couldn't care less about me coming home."

"Chas, you know I'm not used to being alone. I'm just trying to handle it the best I know how."

Feeling sheepish and insecure, in the way I sometimes did, I tried to make things better. "Baby, I'm going to be home in less than forty-eight hours. I'm sure as soon as we see each other it'll be like I never left. All your defense mechanisms will just melt away."

"I'm sure you're right," she answered. "Listen, I gotta get going. Judy's going to be here in less than an hour, and I haven't even started cooking yet."

"OK, baby. Have you got all my flight info?"

"Yeah, I've got everything. I'll meet you outside

baggage claim, OK? I love you, and I'll see you soon."

"I love you too, J.L."

When I got off the phone I still felt upset, so I pulled out my guitar and started to play. After a while, I decided to write a song. I hadn't written a song on my own from start to finish for years, but I came up with what I thought was a really good one. It concerned the mixed emotions I felt about my career and my being away from Joan. "I thought I'd be happy living out my dreams..." it began, and concluded with, "The only place I want to be / Is under the stars with you." "Under the stars" was a secret code between Joan and me. A couple of months before I'd left for England, we'd covered the bedroom ceiling with glow-in-the-dark stars and planets. When we were out somewhere and yearned to be home together, we'd say something like, "I'd much rather be with you under the stars."

All I wanted to do was be at home, under the stars, with my girlfriend. That's what made me happy. I was amazed at how much I missed her.

FIVE

The plane ride back from London took an eternity. Once we landed, customs took even longer. I finally made it through the endless line, and there was Joan, looking as beautiful as ever. Almost immediately, Joan warmed up to me, and the fears I had in London vanished.

As soon as we got home, I played and sang for Joan the song I'd written. We were sitting on the living room couch, and she rocked in time with the music. When I finished, she had a little tear in her eye.

"I love it," she said. "No one's ever done something like that for me."

"Well, with a little luck, someday you'll hear it on the radio and tell people that it's your song," I smiled.

After our happy reunion, Joan and I quickly slipped back into our normal life together, throwing backyard barbecues and enjoying the hot summer in the San Fernando Valley.

Shortly after my return, I learned that our album

release in the United States had been pushed back until the fall. Geffen Records thought we'd be more likely to get airplay if we waited until the market wasn't as saturated by well-known groups with new records. But this turn of events frustrated us, since it had taken us so long to finish the record. We finally had our act together and yet our record wasn't in stores. The more I thought about it, though, the more my disappointment turned to relief. The delay just meant I'd have one more break before my life got really crazy.

Joan and I had planned to take a trip to Hawaii, but she came down with what seemed to be the flu, so we decided to stay closer to home and go to Aspen. We planned to drive there in my black Nissan 240SX and stay at my mom's house. We even decided to take along our Indian ring-necked parrot, Jude, who made a lot of noise and loved french fries. We figured he'd brighten up the drive when he let out a wolf whistle or trilled out the six notes that precede the cheer "Charge!"

It took us two days to reach Aspen, with me doing most of the driving. Joan felt a little better before we left, but she still wasn't up to snuff—she was achy, low on energy, and had a slight fever. We still thought she was just fighting off a virus.

The first thing we did in Aspen was take a relaxing bubble bath together in my mom's tub with its gorgeous view of the mountains. Perhaps that would help speed Joan's recovery. The next day, I took her to my favorite fishing spot in the world—a man-made reservoir nestled in the mountains, which you can reach only by a dirt road. It's unbelievably beautiful, and the reservoir is stocked with trout. I'd never fished there without making a catch, and this day was no different. But while I was catching my limit, Joan sat on a blanket under an umbrella, feeling ill. That night I cooked the trout for us, but she couldn't enjoy it because she was feeling worse and worse.

We thought maybe it was the altitude—the town of Aspen is situated at 8,000 feet. My aunt would sometimes get heart palpitations up there, so we always brought an oxygen tank for her to take a few hits of pure oxygen. There wasn't a tank there now, however, so we phoned Joan's doctor, Barry Rosenbloom, to see if he thought it was a good idea for us to get her one. But considering her symptoms, he told us that it might be the cancer making Joan sick, not the flu.

We hadn't even considered that possibility. Barry, an oncologist and hematologist, perhaps mentioned it when Joan first came down with the "flu," but when she started to feel better he dropped the notion. Looking back, I wonder why he didn't ask her to come in right away for tests, just to rule out the possibility of a cancer relapse. But when you've been seeing a doctor for a while and develop a close relationship, perhaps a certain denial factor sets in. Maybe Barry didn't want to imagine that Joan was facing cancer again just as much as we didn't.

I took Joan to see a doctor in Aspen whom Barry referred us to, and she ran some tests. They came back positive. Not only had Joan's cancer returned, but it had changed from a small-celled type—which responds well to treatment—to a large-celled, very aggressive malignancy. When Barry received the results, he asked us to come back to Los Angeles immediately for more tests. It was likely that Joan would have to start a regimen of very strong intravenous chemotherapy rather than simply take pills, Barry told us.

We were both freaked out by the diagnosis, even though Barry tried to reassure us that he had a success rate of ninety percent with the type of chemotherapy he planned to use on this particular form of cancer. What disturbed me the most was the thought of Joan suffering the side effects of traditional chemo. I knew that losing her hair would be awful for her, since Joan loved looking pretty and feminine. She was a bit of a princess, and being bald didn't fit that picture.

To cheer her up, that afternoon while she was resting I visited my favorite store in Aspen, Fast Eddie's, which specializes in cowboy hats. Aspen is a cowboy-hat sort of town, and I love wearing them, so I decided to get Joan one too. I figured that after undergoing chemo she'd be wearing a lot of different head coverings for a while. She liked the hat I bought her a lot and appreciated my efforts to make her feel better, but she still felt lousy and apprehensive.

Barry wanted us in Los Angeles the next day, but that was a problem since we'd come in my car and with a parrot. Frantic about what to do, I phoned my mom in Los Angeles. Her assistant Deb picked up, then quickly transferred the call.

"Hi, Da," my mom said. (That was my childhood nickname, derived from my baby brother calling me "Da-dee-da.") "Is Aspen beautiful? Are you having a great time?"

Choking up, I blurted out, "No, Joan's really sick. Her doctor sent her to get tests here, and her cancer's gotten really bad. He wants us to come back right away."

"Oh, Da, I'm so sorry."

I started to cry. "I don't know what we're going to do, because we drove my car here."

"Don't worry about that. I'll get you both booked on a flight back first thing tomorrow morning."

"What about the car?"

"I'll find someone to drive it back."

"I'm really scared, Mom. Joan is so sick, and Barry's worried that the cancer has gone into her bone marrow. What if she dies?"

"Whoa!" She stopped me. "You're really jumping ahead. Just take it as it comes. Don't worry about that unless you have to. Wait and see what Barry has to say."

"I know...you're right. I'm just losing it."

"I understand." She paused. "But let's just take it one step at a time. I'm going to get off the phone now and make some calls. I'll have Deb call you back with your flight info."

"Thanks, Mom. I love you."

"I love you too."

My mom always comes through in a pinch—she's calm and rational when someone else is feeling bad or scared. I really appreciate her at those times. When I was a kid, she was the kind of parent who wouldn't get hysterical if I came in bleeding from a fall. She'd just say, "You're OK, you're OK—let's just get you to the doctor."

Shortly after arriving in Los Angeles, Joan and I went to see Barry, who ordered more blood tests and performed a bone-marrow biopsy. That required him to make an incision in Joan's lower back, insert an instrument that looks like a key to a wind-up toy, then crank it into her bone and extract the marrow through it . With the instrument in her back, for a moment Joan looked like a human toy.

The results revealed just what Barry had feared: The cancer had spread to her bone marrow, which explained her achiness and low-grade fever. Barry made an appointment for Joan to start chemotherapy the next day. She would receive four to six rounds of the medication, one dose every three or four weeks. The chemo was so strong that it would take her body that long to recover between treatments.

The next day at the doctor's office, we were given a private room instead of having to go to the "chemo room," which is filled with a number of other people in recliner chairs taking chemo. I guess Barry wanted to make the session easier for us. A nurse put the IV into Joan's arm and connected it to a bag of saline solution and antinausea medication. Then she attached the bag of chemo to the stand and started the drip into Joan's veins. It was emotionally overwhelming for me to watch. The chemo didn't look any different than the saline or the other medicine, but I thought it should. I wanted it to be red or green to distinguish itself and point out the damage and pain it would cause. But no, it was just a clear liquid. I was horrified watching the first drops ease their way down from the bag, through the tubing, getting closer and closer to the needle in Joan's arm, eventually finding their way into her bloodstream.

It took hours to slowly infuse all the chemo inside her. There was no backing out of the course we'd embarked upon, because the poison was now within Joan's body. We were sent home with an oral antinausea medication for her to take. It worked like a charm, and Joan never became nauseous from the chemo. Thank God for small favors.

Joan's hair didn't fall out right away—it takes a couple of weeks after chemo for that to happen. At this point, hair loss was the most traumatic thing we were expecting, since Barry had been so optimistic about the chemo putting her into remission. I was really flipped out about her losing her hair, both because Joan's physical appearance meant so much to her and because I was afraid of how it might affect *my* feelings. Would I still be attracted to her? I felt guilty for even having such thoughts. I knew I'd be able to handle whatever came up, but I was scared of the changes that were sure to happen—scared that I would look at her differently, and not in a good way.

It was suggested that Joan get a haircut before her hair started to fall out, since it would be more empowering for her. A person's hair doesn't fall out all at once from chemo, but slowly over the course of a few months. So it's supposedly less traumatic to lose your hair when it's already short, as opposed to having long strands fall out. It also looks better, because the hair loss isn't as obvious.

Joan called up well-known Beverly Hills hairdresser José Eber, who was a good friend of hers and my family. He turned out to be a prince. We went to his house for the haircut, and he was very reassuring as he snipped off her past-shoulder-length hair. Joan hadn't worn her hair short since she was a baby, but Jose created an attractive and stylish short cut. I couldn't believe how good it looked. That simple haircut went a long way toward relieving the anxiety both of us were feeling.

Joan's symptoms vanished almost immediately after her first round of chemo. She felt great. "I don't know why people say chemotherapy is so bad!" she told me. We felt very optimistic, as did her doctor.

About a week after she began treatment, we ventured out to Laguna Beach for a few days. Aspen, after all, hadn't been the getaway we'd hoped for. Our time at the beach was peaceful, except for one night when Joan woke up crying.

"What's wrong?" I said, jolted from a deep sleep.

"Everything."

"You're gonna be OK." I wrapped her in my arms. "Look at how much better you're already feeling."

"I know, I know, but I just can't believe I have to go through this."

"I hate that you have to go through this, Joan, but four months from now this will all be behind us."

"Baby, just hold me," she said, pulling me closer.

I felt confident about her recovery, since the chemo was working better than anyone had expected. The only thing bothering me was that Ceremony had a promotional tour of radio stations scheduled, which meant I'd be away from Joan for three weeks. I wouldn't even be there for her second round of chemo. She did plan to visit me in Atlanta, though, where I'd have a weekend off. But that wasn't much consolation.

The next week, Rachel and I set out for New York along with Nick, our new guitarist (the other one had moved away). We liked Nick a lot—he seemed more on our side than our other band members. But the radio station tour proved to be even more difficult and disheartening than making the album had been.

This was a typical day: We'd visit the early morning radio drive-time show in whatever city we were in, play a song or two live in their studio, do an interview, then immediately get on a plane and go to the next city. There, we'd have lunch with the personnel from the radio station and play a song on their afternoon drive-time show. After that we'd hop on another plane and fly to yet another city, where we'd have dinner with the radio people whose show we were scheduled on the next morning. It was crazy.

The tour was designed to get radio stations excited about our record and encourage them to play the single, so not only did we have to perform and do interviews but we had to kiss the asses of the station programmers and managers. That's what every other band in the business did, so our efforts didn't evoke any sort of appreciation or gratitude. It was all about, "What can you do for *us?*" Rachel and I were required to always be "on" and obliging, whether it was signing albums for every person they knew, having drinks with them, or eating whatever dish off a restaurant menu they wanted us to try. I made the mistake of yawning in front of one radio guy and he got annoyed. "What, are you tired?" he asked. As if I had the right to be tired while visiting his radio station! The whole tour was designed for us to make these people feel special for the few hours we spent with them. Our needs didn't figure into the equation at all.

At a small station in Florida we had a particularly bizarre experience. After guesting on a show, we went out to lunch with the program director, who was a backwater type of guy. He regaled us with his theory that Madonna was going to die young—tragically and dramatically—like Marilyn Monroe. To prepare for the big event, he'd gotten some posters of her album *True Blue*— "Which *is* blue," he informed us in his Southern drawl.

He said he planned to get the posters signed by her. "I'm gonna make me a collector's series," he told us, "so when she dies tragically and dramatically like Marilyn Monroe, they'll be worth a lot of money."

After we left him, we couldn't stop talking about how psycho he was. For months afterward, we keep expecting to read that Madonna had been shot by Sam the Program Manager, from Backwater, Florida. When we found out later that he was a convicted child molester, we weren't surprised. These were the kind of people we spent time with. I think they resented that all they got was our attention—not any of the old-time radio payola of money and cocaine and prostitutes. I felt dirty after each day of promoting ourselves, as if I were a prostitute.

We ended the first week of our press tour in Atlanta, and Joan flew in as planned. No one could have imagined how sick she was from how terrific she looked—healthy and vibrant. Like her old self. She'd lost a few pounds, but that just put her at what she considered her ideal weight.

We stayed at a Four Seasons hotel in the suburb of Buckhead, with the record company picking up our tab. Joan was feeling great, even though her hair had started to fall out. It wasn't like she woke up with her pillow covered with hair, but if she pulled on her hair it would come out in her hand. She was resigned to it, she said, and the loss didn't show yet, but when she washed or brushed her hair, she'd do so very gently.

By this time, Rachel and Joan were civil to each other but still resentful—Joan toward Rachel for the way she'd manipulated me into staying with her and for banning her from rehearsals, and Rachel toward Joan because of her part in our breakup. They didn't want to see each other, so Rachel spent most of the weekend in her hotel room while Joan and I hung out with Nick and Amy's brother Adam, who was gay and lived in Atlanta. Adam and his lover Jim took us around town, cooked dinner for us at their house, and showed us that famous Southern hospitality.

The first night of Joan's visit, we spent the entire evening in bed, ordering room service, catching up, and making love. We shut the whole world out for the night, which was exactly what we both needed. Since Joan's relapse, we'd had sex only a few times, but that weekend we made love like we used to. We were serious rather than playful, focusing less on the physicality of sex and more on our feelings for each other. Having sex was now a true act of love, compassion, and caring.

Joan's illness was definitely changing me. I was growing up very quickly. Too quickly. My life with Joan had been great so far, and I wanted to believe that her illness would only give me a richer perspective. Perhaps I was living in some kind of denial, but I was still planning on being with Joan for a long, long time. I imagined she'd probably die of cancer at some point—just not now. I was only twenty-four years old, and I thought we both were invincible. I didn't admit the possibility of any other scenario. As far as I was concerned, the worst was already over. We'd just get through this setback, and then life would return to normal.

That Monday morning, Joan took a cab to the airport, and Rachel and I went off to make an appearance at a radio station in Atlanta. Sadly, that weekend with Joan turned out to be the last "normal" time we'd ever spend together.

*

During the last week of the promo tour, Joan's symptoms returned. She phoned to say she was feeling really sick again—achy, feverish, weak. I told her I loved her and missed her, but it was all I could do. It was hard for me to be away while she felt like this. As the week wore on, she told me she wasn't feeling any better, so I called her doctor.

"Is it normal for her to feel this way, Barry? What's going on?"

He couldn't reassure me, as I had hoped, because he was also concerned about Joan's recurring symptoms. This time he expressed a little less optimism about her chances of recovery. At first he'd said Joan had a ninety percent chance of getting better; now he was talking about a seventy percent chance. I was getting very worried.

That weekend, Rachel and I were in Chicago with some free time to ourselves. Her new girlfriend had come for a visit, but I was too preoccupied with Joan's health to spend much time with them. One weekend night, the Geffen Records promotion person on that leg of the tour—a lesbian with whom we'd developed a friendly rapport—wanted to take the three of us out to a nice dinner and then to a gay club. I went along but wasn't in a mood to socialize. Instead I met a woman at the club who was a nurse, and we spent the evening talking about cancer.

The next day, during which I was free to roam the city, I ended up at an alternative bookstore where I bought books about cancer. Nothing could take my mind off it. One of the books was a woman's personal memoir about her recovery from breast cancer, in which the author recounted the horrors of undergoing a stem-cell transplant. *Thank God Joan won't have to go through that*, I thought, since Barry had never mentioned that possibility.

The idea that Joan might die soon had begun to cross my mind. At one point that weekend, while taking a shower, I started to pray. I wasn't raised with any religion, and I was never much for prayer, but I didn't know what else to do. I prayed that my role would be to help Joan fight and overcome her illness. But I also prayed, "If it's not meant for her to beat it, help me accept that reality and let me be there for her transition out of this life." I had read Raymond Moody's book *Life After Life* before Joan and I had gotten together, and that's where I'd come across that concept.

Back in L.A., Joan wasn't handling the situation very well. Some people face illness with a strong fighting spirit; Joan felt crushed by it. She was stuck in a "Why me?" space, and I was just as worried about her emotional state as her physical one. One day when I called her from the road, she sounded particularly upset.

"Hi, baby, how are you feeling?" I said.

"I'm feeling terrible," she told me, "worse than before I started the chemo."

"I'm so sorry I can't be there with you—did you call Barry?"

"I'm seeing him tomorrow for my second round."

"I'm sure the chemo will have you feeling good again in no time. Just try and get through the next couple of days."

"Chas, I don't know if I can take this." Her voice sounded defeated, and she was weepy.

"Honey, you don't have a choice—you have to take it."

"I just feel so awful, and it seems like it's been going on for so long now. I don't know how much longer I can stand it. I'm starting to think that it might not be worth it. I'm probably going to die in the end anyway."

I was scared to hear this and felt helpless because I wasn't there with her. If I were, at least I could take care of the simple household tasks, and she could concentrate on getting better. I wanted to be able to watch over her; I was afraid she'd do something to herself.

"Baby, please don't talk that way," I said. "You've got to be strong now. I'll be home in a couple of days, and I'll help you get through this. Just hold on until then. *Please.*"

"I'll try," she said.

"Joan, I've got to go now. But I'm going to call Scotti and tell her to come over and sit with you. I'll call you in a few hours. I love you very much."

"I love you too."

Scotti was in the middle of watching a baseball game when I called and didn't seem enthused about getting right up. "Yeah, sure, Chas, I'll be over there in a little while—as soon as my game's over."

Joan later told me that Scotti hadn't come over for about an hour. I thought she should have dropped everything immediately and gone over to care for Joan, but in defense of Scotti, she had long heard Joan express suicidal thoughts over *breakups,* so she was more used to her changing moods. Scotti was also in denial about how sick Joan really was; I think she was having a hard time dealing with her "child" being ill. Joan wasn't being neglected exactly, but I considered myself the only one who could truly care for her.

Before I returned home, Joan went in for her second round of chemo, which made her feel better again. We were all relieved. I figured she just needed two doses of chemo this time. But when I came home, I immediately noticed how unhealthy she looked—skinnier, older, and with much of her hair gone. Obviously the chemo had worn her down, but I tried to focus on the fact that she felt better rather than how she looked.

One day Joan even felt strong enough to go shopping with Donna and me on Melrose, a street in West Hollywood full of boutiques. As we passed the novelty sex shop Drake's, Donna suggested we stop in; she wanted a new vibrator. Joan and I got a good laugh over the various toys in the shop while Donna made her purchase.

Our next stop was a clothing store where Donna and Joan tried on jeans. As we left, a flamboyantly gay salesman came running out after us.

"Yoo-hoo, girls, you forgot something!"

It was Donna's new vibrator. By the smirking tone of the guy's voice, it was obvious that he'd peeked into the bag.

"Oh, great, Donna," I said. "You know how things are in my life—it's going to come out in the tabloids next week that Chastity Bono left her vibrator in a clothing store on Melrose!"

We all laughed about this, but wouldn't you know it, the next week someone came up to Donna at E! Television where she worked and said, "I've got the *best* Chastity Bono story!" Sure enough, it was about the vibrator. Fortunately, this person knew I was Donna's friend and wasn't about to take the story to the tabloids.

After that weekend I was the one who started feeling sick. I had a fever, I was achy, I couldn't get out of bed, and my throat was so sore I couldn't swallow. The first doctor I saw thought I had mono and gave me a test for it, but it came up negative. I found out later that the test sometimes gives false negatives. Both that doctor and a second one prescribed antibiotics, but nothing made me feel better. A third doctor finally confirmed that I had mono and an ulcerated throat—which he at first thought was herpes, contracted by having oral sex with men.

"That's impossible," I told him. "I'm gay."

He then helped set me on the road to recovery with a different type of antibiotic, homeopathic drops, acupuncture, and intravenous doses of vitamin C.

Meanwhile, a week and a half after her second round of chemo, Joan got sick again. I was really worried about her catching mono from me—chemotherapy seriously compromises the immune system—so although we were staying together we weren't being intimate. But since I was sick, neither of us could care for the other one. We ended up spending a week at my mom's house in Malibu, where she (and her cook and housekeepers) took good care of both of us. My mom had always been good at playing doctor, making sure I took my medicine on time, or waking up to be with me if I got sick in the middle of the night.

While we stayed at her house, my mom spent time talking with us, letting us know how bad she felt about what Joan was going through. Although it could have been really awkward—hosting her old friend who was now her daughter's lover—it wasn't. We were comfortable being with my mom, even if I wasn't ready to be openly affectionate with Joan in front of her.

＊

In the midst of these health crises, the promotion for Ceremony's record continued. The news so far, however, was lousy. Despite all our efforts and ass-kissing, our record wasn't being played. None of the radio stations we visited had added it to their play lists. At one big station, the program director—who loved the record—got fired. It just wasn't happening for us, but we were told it was still early in the promotional process.

As soon as I started to feel the slightest bit better, Rachel and I flew to New York to do *Regis and Kathy Lee* and another network morning show. I was still really weak, since mono is the kind of illness that, even once you're not deathly ill, makes you so weak that you get winded after walking half a block.

We were staying at the Paramount Hotel, a hip, rock-star sort of place where the furniture is weird, angular stuff out of a Tim Burton movie and the bedroom is the size of a closet. I didn't care about the hotel's cool decor—I wanted some *space*, because I get really claustrophobic in small hotel rooms. It was particularly hard for me to be in such a small room because I was stuck there most of the day, feeling too sick to do anything after appearing on TV.

Before one of the shows, I was extremely sick and suffering from the chills. There were no other warm things around, so I wrapped myself in a furniture blanket and somehow managed to make it through.

Afterward, the producer said, "I don't know how you did that!"

The best thing about *Regis and Kathy Lee* was that the cohost subbing for Kathy Lee was Carol Burnett. Her show had been shot on the same lot as *The Sonny and Cher Show*, and she had always been very nice to me. I just wished I hadn't felt so crappy, since I might have actually enjoyed myself for an hour.

Right before we left New York, we were booked at a huge radio promotion show outside the city. There were about 10,000 people at the free outdoor event, where various pop and dance bands either lip-synched or performed to backing tracks. Ceremony, however, was performing live with acoustic guitars. Imagine Joan Baez on the same bill with Mariah Carey or Janet Jackson—that's what it was like. The weather didn't help either, since it was a cold, early October night and I was still sick. My voice was scratchy, and it was hard for me to hit certain notes. At one point I accidentally whacked the mike stand with my guitar and it made a loud crack. All in all, it was the most horrifying stage experience I'd ever have.

By the time I got home, I was as sick as I'd been before I left, so I had to start a round of treatments all over again. No one had even considered that we should have postponed the promo trip. In the music business, nobody cares. The attitude is, "What's the problem? Why aren't you up to speed? You have mono? So what?" You're hurt, you still play.

Joan was also still sick. After each round of chemo, the window of improvement got shorter and shorter. First she felt better for two weeks, then a week and a half, then just a week. It was becoming more and more apparent that the chemo wasn't working, but the doctors wanted to continue the regimen nonetheless.

Finally, I said to Barry one day at his office, "Before you give her more chemo, don't you think you should test her bone marrow again and see what's going on?" He agreed.

Before the bone marrow extraction, Joan received a very strong tranquilizer that heavily sedated her but didn't put her to sleep. This particular drug has some other strange side effects: It leaves the patient with amnesia about what's gone on and acts like a sort of truth serum. Plus, it removes inhibitions. Whatever was on Joan's mind before she was given the drug she would talk about, uncensored. That's what had happened the last time she'd been given it, so weren't surprised when it happened again.

This time, though, right before she was given the drug, Joan and I made the mistake of talking about how much we missed having sex, which had become nonexistent while she was receiving chemo. You can guess what happened when the tranquilizer kicked in: Joan started describing in detail what she missed the most about sex! I wasn't the only one in the room either, since nurses were constantly walking in and out. I tried to cover Joan's mouth, or talk loudly to the nurses, or just shush her, but she wouldn't shut up. She was hell-bent on sharing every private thought with me, oblivious to everyone around us.

We'd also been talking about Barry before she was given the drug, commenting on what a good relationship we had developed with him. When he came in to extract the bone marrow, Joan was lying on her side with her hand hanging a bit off the examining table. As he walked up to her, he accidentally brushed his crotch against her hand, and Joan, in her drugged stupor, got a devilish look on her face. She suddenly reached out, grabbed his dick, and started laughing hysterically. It certainly took the edge off the procedure, as both Barry and I cracked up as well.

After about twenty minutes, the test was over and Joan came out of her haze. Since she knew about the drug's typical effects, the first thing out of her mouth was, "Did I do or say anything I should know about?"

"You're not going to believe what you said this time," I smirked.

She thought I was kidding when I told her some of the explicit things she'd said in earshot of the nurses. Then I told her that she'd grabbed Barry.

"I didn't!" Joan said, mortified.

"Oh yes, you did."

Barry came back in at that point, and he and I started howling all over again. It was one of the best laughs I'd had during that awful time.

But the amusement was short-lived. The test showed there were more cancer cells in Joan's marrow than before, which was devastating news. The next day at Barry's office, we discussed our options. He could try other chemotherapy regimens, but there was little evidence that they'd be any more effective. Before Joan and I became completely disheartened, though, he offered another possibility: The disease might be cured with a stem-cell transplant. Until now, Barry had never used the word "cure" with us. He'd always spoken in terms of treating the disease and putting Joan into remission. When he'd diagnosed her four years before, he'd said there was no cure for non-Hodgkin's lymphoma.

As Barry discussed stem-cell transplants with us, I flashed on the book I'd read a month before. A stem-cell transplant, from what I knew, seemed like the worst treatment anyone could undergo. But Barry had used the word "cure." For a cure, Joan and I were willing to go to hell and back.

And that's basically where we'd go.

SIX

Even after reading that book by the woman who survived breast cancer, I still wasn't clear on what a stem-cell transplant actually entailed, but Barry explained it to us. All of the body's blood cells are produced in the bone marrow, he said, and the youngest of those blood cells are called stem cells. As the stem cells mature, they become whatever kind of blood cell your body needs—white cells (for fighting infection), red cells (for transporting oxygen), or platelets (for clotting). A stem-cell transplant rebuilds the bone marrow after it's been destroyed by a very high dose of chemotherapy—a dose high enough to knock out the most resistant cancer cells.

The first step in a transplant is to harvest stem cells by drawing out the patient's blood, running it through a machine that extracts the stem cells, then returning the rest of the blood to the body. There aren't a lot of stem cells in the blood, so it takes several long procedures to extract a sufficient number for the transplant. Joan would have to be "harvested" three or four times.

As a precautionary measure, in case something happened to the stem cells while they were being preserved and stored, the doctors would also harvest bone marrow from Joan and transplant that as well, which would then produce new cells. It would be better, though, just to transplant the stem cells directly—like buying starter plants at the nursery instead of seeds.

The second step, after the cells are harvested, is to bombard the patient with enough chemotherapy to essentially kill all the blood cells and all the bone marrow. Joan would be left without an immune system, temporarily, which of course would put her at a lot of risk. After twenty-four to forty-eight hours, the chemo itself passes out of the patient's body—though the cells continue to die—and that's when the stem cells are reinfused. If Joan were given those high doses of different types of chemotherapy and not given stem cells, she wouldn't survive.

After that, all you can do is wait and pray. You pray that the chemo has destroyed the cancer cells, and you pray that the stem cells create a whole new blood, bone marrow, and immune system before an infection can take full advantage of the body's powerless condition.

Barry let us know all the possible side effects Joan faced, starting with the worst: death. But since he'd said the "C" word to us, we weren't too concerned about the five percent chance of her dying from the procedure. We figured that those who died from it were older or sicker than Joan. Since her disease supposedly didn't have a cure, we were ready to do anything for the possibility of one. If Barry had told us to jump off the Empire State Building, we might have done it. The stem-cell transplant was the only chance Joan had been given, so we were taking it.

✳

Around this time, Joan and I went to see Rosalyn Bruyere, a world-renowned psychic healer. Ellen Burstyn's character in the 1980 movie *Resurrection* was based on her. My grandmother had read about Rosalyn in *Psychology Today* and had attended one of her weekend seminars. Later, when she had gone through a bout of diverticulitis, she called Rosalyn, who came to the hospital and laid her hands on her. The doctors had planned to operate if my grandmother's condition didn't improve, but the next day she was fine and they released her. So Rosalyn—a tall, heavyset woman in her forties with long thick hair, a sweet face, and a voice "like tinkling bells," as my grandma put it—had become a friend of the family. We hoped she'd be able to work her healing powers on Joan.

As Joan lay on a massage table, Rosalyn put her hands on her. She didn't say anything; she just moved her hands from place to place, mostly around Joan's abdomen, for perhaps fifteen minutes. Afterward, though, Rosalyn seemed to be paying more attention to me than to Joan. She asked Joan to lie there and relax, and took me on a walk around her grounds. She asked me how I was handling everything and let me know that if I needed anything, she was there for me. At the time I thought she was just a wonderfully caring person. When I looked back on it later, though, I realized she was trying to prepare me for the worst. I think she believed, from work-ing with her, that Joan's illness could be terminal.

The healing session didn't seem to help Joan. In fact, before the transplant took place, Joan began suffering tremendous abdominal pain, and the doctors didn't know what was causing it. Barry decided to put her on mor-phine and taught me how to inject her with it. That first night after we were given the morphine, Joan woke up screaming bloody murder, begging me to make the pain stop. I had just learned how to do the injection, and I was shaking trying to fill up the syringe and give her the shot. I'd soon become an expert at it.

Over the next couple of days, Joan continued to be in terrible pain despite the drugs, so Barry suggested she check into the hospital. She resisted until he finally told her, "You're going into the hospital. It's no longer your decision. We need to find out what's going on."

So Joan checked into Cedars-Sinai in West Hollywood. It was scary being in the hospital, even though we both thought it would just be a brief stay. Joan's room was on the fourth floor, the oncology ward, which was a particu-larly depressing place because everyone there had cancer and looked extremely sick. When I first walked down the long hospital hallways looking for ice and food machines, I couldn't help peering into room after room after room. Everyone kept their doors open, and I saw many old, sick, lonely people in hospital gowns. It was terribly sad.

The doctors gave Joan a battery of tests to find the source of her pain, and it turned out that the lymph nodes in her belly were enlarged and tumorous. By now she was very sick—I couldn't even fathom how sick she was, since denial had become such a huge part of this experience for me. But the transplant specialist from Barry's office, Dr. Sheldon Goldstein, quickly knocked me out of denial. He informed us that the stem-cell transplant couldn't be performed while Joan was this ill. First she'd have to go through a few more rounds of a different type of chemo, to put her back into at least a temporary remission.

"If that doesn't work," Dr. Goldstein said flatly, "there's nothing more we can do for her."

He said this in front of Joan, with no softening in his tone, and then left the room. So much for a pleasant bedside manner.

Perhaps Joan was in too much pain or too stoned on drugs for this to register, but somehow it didn't faze her. I was in total shock. I not only couldn't believe the doctor's insensitivity, but I couldn't believe what he'd just said. I was so upset that I had to leave the hospital for a while so Joan wouldn't notice.

I went to Rachel's house and cried on her shoulder, allowing myself to feel completely devastated for a few moments. I couldn't afford to remain pessimistic. I couldn't afford to believe the treatment wouldn't work. Even if it wasn't based on anything but desire, I still had to maintain hope. I couldn't accept the possibility that Joan might die.

The next day, Joan began a new regimen of IV chemo. This time she was anesthetized and the doctors installed in her chest a Hickman catheter—a tube that goes into the main artery but hangs out of the body. Through it, nurses could draw blood and inject IV medications and transfusions without having to look for a vein each time.

As for the chemo injection itself, Joan and I already

felt like old hats. I was terrified it wouldn't work, though, because we'd been told it was Joan's last chance. Fortunately, it did its job, killing the cancer cells and making her feel better, but it also dramatically brought down her blood counts. Joan was now considered neutropenic, which means she had a very low white blood-cell count and was thus susceptible to infections from viruses and bacteria that normally have no effect because they're blocked by the immune system.

To help protect her from infection, Joan couldn't have any flowers or plants in her room, she was forbidden to eat any raw vegetables or fruit, and she could only eat meat that was cooked well done. Visitors had to wash their hands before coming in to see her. She also received constant transfusions of blood and platelets, along with various medications, to try to stimulate her bone marrow to produce new white and red blood cells. The hospital encouraged us to ask our friends donate blood and platelets for her, which they generously did.

Joan's supposedly brief stay at the hospital turned into a month-long residency. I was with her constantly, sleeping on a cot in her room (every room at Cedars is private). José Eber, who lived in the neighborhood, arranged for his favorite local Italian restaurant to deliver food whenever we wanted and to put it on his bill. Because she was neutropenic, Joan was restricted to hospital food, so that left the good stuff for me. Other than the food from Jose, the hospital was a lousy place for a healthy person to be. It was boring, it wasn't restful (nurses came into the room all night long), and above all, it was depressing.

Over the course of that month, I became very close with some of the nurses, who tried to take care of both

Joan and me. Seeing how bloodshot and dark-circled my eyes had become, they sometimes sent me away, saying, "Go home and let us do our work for a night, OK?" They just wanted me to get a good night's sleep. At first the staff didn't quite know what to make of me, though. I got quite a laugh when Barry told me that one of the nurses had said, "Joan's daughter sure looks a lot like Chastity Bono."

After a while, I started to look more like Joan's mother. My own mom jokingly told me that I had started to resemble Shirley MacLaine in *Terms of Endearment*. Like her character in the movie, whose daughter is in the hospital with cancer, I looked haggard and my hair desperately needed coloring, since my dark-blond roots were now two inches long.

One night at the hospital, Joan woke up in a panic, screaming, "I've got to get out of here! I've got to get out of here!" She tried to leave her bed despite her being hooked up to IVs through the Hickman—which would have created a bloody mess if they had come out. Knowing this, I jumped up from my cot, pinned her to the bed, and yelled for help. As nurses and doctors came rushing in, Joan was in a state of total delirium, her face beet red. She didn't even know who I was. I was terrified that she would never return to normal.

The medical staff held her down and gave her a fast-acting sedative, then assessed what was happening. Their exam showed that she had a 104-degree fever, her blood pressure had dropped, her pulse was erratic, and she was severely dehydrated. She had even urinated on herself. The doctors speculated that she'd contracted a sudden infection that had spiked her fever, and the fever had led to her dehydration.

They injected her with bags of saline solution, and after a few hours Joan emerged from her wild state, but she had no recollection of what had occurred. It was like she had just "come to" and now calmly wondered why everyone was gathered around her making such a big deal.

The doctors put Joan in the ICU for a few days after this, and the crisis passed. I could have used some intensive care myself at this point, because I felt like a total wreck. Instead I had to fly to Flint, Michigan, to play yet another radio-sponsored concert. I didn't want to go, nor did Rachel and Nick. Rachel knew that all the radio shows we'd done had been awful, and Nick was pissed off that our manager owed him money. I just didn't want to leave Joan. Besides, our single had been out since the beginning of September and it was now late October, so the record company was no longer promoting it very much. We figured that somebody at Geffen owed somebody in Flint a favor and that was the only reason we were being shipped out there.

On top of all that, who on earth wanted to go to Flint, Michigan? I'd seen the documentary *Roger and Me*, so when I thought of Flint all I could imagine was the woman who sells rabbits "for pets or meat." We were all so depressed about the trip that while we were in the limo on our way to the Los Angeles airport, we almost asked the driver to turn around and take us back. But we didn't.

After we arrived in Flint, the first signs were inauspicious: We were booked at a crappy motel, our sound check didn't go well, and the headlining act was The Village People. I could have gotten a kick out of being on the same bill as The Village People, except I figured their audience wouldn't be grooving to *our* music as well. We were preparing ourselves for disappointment at best, disaster at worst.

The show was in a conference center attached to a hotel, and the place was packed with about a thousand people. It was the day before Halloween, so everyone was wearing costumes. We even had to judge a local costume contest before we played. Then came the surprise of our lives: As we went onstage and Nick played the opening riff of our single "Could Have Been Love," the crowd actually started cheering. In fact, they were going crazy! We all turned around to see if some famous person had come onstage behind us, but nobody was there. They were screaming for us! What the hell was going on?

When I started singing, the audience grew even louder. People were even singing along with me! They knew the words to our song! Rachel and Nick and I looked at one another, then at the audience, then back at one another with goofy grins on our faces. The crowd went wild at the chorus and even wilder as we started the next verse. It was as if we were playing a hit record.

The audience was still cheering for us during the next two songs, even though they weren't familiar with them. As we left the stage, we asked someone from the radio station, "How do they know our song? What's going on?"

"Your song was a big hit in this area," he told us. "We played it all the time on our station."

No one had told us this. I guess our record company thought it was no big deal how our record was doing in Flint, Michigan. But it was a big deal to us, considering how poorly everything else was going with our record. It would have been nice knowing *someone* liked us.

As we walked back to our motel, we experienced another perk of our sudden Flint stardom: A bunch of lesbian groupies were waiting for us! They were all in their Halloween costumes, including one girl dressed as a soldier, who gave me a fake hand grenade as a present. The entire lesbian community of Flint, Michigan, must have been hanging around outside our rooms. This was just wild, and Rachel and I were really excited. Even Nick was having a good time, although he wasn't about to score with this crowd.

Thinking we were utter failures in our recording career, we'd now discovered that people in one small corner of the country knew and loved us. It was the best gig the record company had sent us on, and we almost hadn't gone. For the three minutes and however many seconds we were playing "Could Have Been Love," I felt like a huge success. So that's what a hit song feels like, I realized: cute young girls staring up adoringly at you from the front row, singing along not just with the choruses but with the verses too.

✳

The buzz from our Flint experience lasted a while, but Rachel and I soon woke up to the fact that nothing else was happening with the record. Having put so much work into creating and promoting it, we were disappointed to say the least. Then again, part of me was relieved. If the record did take off, I'd have to let someone down—Joan, if I took to the road, or Rachel and the record company if I stayed with Joan. With Joan so sick, I knew I couldn't have given my recording career the focus it would have needed.

I had called Joan from Flint to tell her how great our show had gone, and she was thrilled. The next day I flew back to Los Angeles, and by that afternoon I was at the hospital again, glad to see her but depressed because it was Halloween and we were missing out on celebrating the one night of the year we could be out dancing together. Just a year before, Joan and I had been so happy, having finally cleared away all the people and things in our lives that had kept us apart. Now she was extremely sick, and I was exhausted from caring for her.

I covered up my feelings, though. Everything in my life now was about Joan and her recovery. I didn't even know where to seek support for myself. I tried to get involved with The Wellness Community, a cancer support organization, but Joan wasn't interested in attending a support group. She said being around others with cancer would depress her. I totally disagreed, but Joan's way to handle things was to stay in denial, and I didn't want to push her too hard. The Wellness Community required that the person who had cancer participate in the program, otherwise people in her life couldn't go to the meetings. I didn't know where else to turn, except occasionally to a social worker in the hospital when I could steal a little time away from Joan.

Our friends couldn't offer much support to me either, because they were focused on Joan. I wasn't complaining to anyone about this, because I didn't realize at the time that I even needed or deserved to be cared for. Joan was the sick one; everything had to be directed toward her. It didn't seem appropriate that what I was going through should draw any attention.

Joan had now been in the hospital four weeks, and her blood counts had become stable again, so Barry allowed her to check out. He decided that the next chemo regimen could begin at her home, as long as a nurse came to administer the medication and Joan was regularly monitored to see whether her blood counts stayed up. If she became neutropenic again, she'd have to return to the hospital.

Coming home with her after that month away felt strange. Joan was so much sicker and weaker than she'd been when she had entered the hospital. The chemo had taken a great toll on her, and she was extremely thin and fragile. She now was taking a whole cocktail of drugs intravenously through the Hickman: Dilaudid for pain, Ativan for anxiety and to settle her stomach, and two different medications to increase her production of red and white cells. She had grown very dependent upon me, and my schedule revolved around when she needed her medications, which was every four to six hours. I'd been taught to clean and flush the Hickman and to change Joan's dressing, as well as how to fill syringes and administer injections.

Joan didn't learn how to do any of this herself. One reason was that I wanted to do everything for her; otherwise I felt helpless and out of control. Another was that she was too sick and weak to care for herself. Her eyesight had deteriorated, and her ability to concentrate had decreased. It would have been hard for her to do things with precision.

I also think she didn't want to deal with her own illness. In fact, the Dilaudid only heightened that feeling for her. It's like synthetic heroin; stronger than morphine, it makes you completely stupefied. Besides relieving her physical pain and discomfort, the Dilaudid also relieved some of Joan's emotional pain. She wanted those Dilaudid shots in an addictive way, and I knew it wasn't just because she was hurting. Dilaudid made her feel good; it gave her a rush. It was like shooting heroin, only cleaner.

The fact is, Joan had long been a pothead, smoking marijuana every day. When we were just friends, I hadn't realized how much she smoked or how addictive that drug can be. (It wasn't a drug that I used, except occasionally when Joan and I had sex, because it usually made me feel paranoid.) Once we became a couple, though, I could tell when Joan had smoked, because she became noticeably goofier. When she got sick she cut out pot, saying she had always associated it with having fun. Now that she wasn't having fun, she didn't want to smoke it. Perhaps the Dilaudid, albeit a much stronger drug, served as a replacement of sorts.

If I had thought the hospital was a difficult place to be, I now realized that being home with a very sick person was much worse. At the hospital there were nurses at her beck and call; here it was just me. I was caring for all of Joan's medical needs, making sure both of us ate, keeping the house in order, and feeding three cats and two dogs. I also had to drive Joan to the doctor every other day for transfusions or an exam. The only outside medical assistance she was getting at home was from a nurse who came every day to take her blood. The nurse also administered the next chemo treatment a few days after we got home.

In addition to everything else, I was in charge of keeping up Joan's spirits. Some of our friends dropped by to help out a little, but Scotti wasn't much help. She came over to the house to visit but had rarely come to the hospital. She said it brought up memories of when one of her parents had died. She was clearly having a hard time seeing Joan so sick. Her lack of support was difficult for me, and rather disappointing.

Even though I was completely stressed out, I took some pride in how I was handling this extremely difficult responsibility. I'd been struggling my whole life with low self-esteem; now, thrust into a terrible crisis, I'd risen to the occasion. I was gaining an entirely new perspective on myself, feeling needed and productive. I was caring for the woman I'd loved for nearly half my life. I was as much honored to be in this position as I was overwhelmed by it.

Yet the overwhelmed part sometimes took precedence, and I looked for something to help me cope. The house was now stocked with bottles and bottles of drugs. With Joan's knowledge, I started taking the painkiller Percodan. It was left over from an earlier stage of her illness, when her pain hadn't required something as strong as morphine or Dilaudid. I took one or two Percodans a day—that's all. I wasn't getting out of hand with it, I told myself. I just didn't want to feel much of anything, and I needed to combat the boredom of being home every day caring for my very sick lover. High on Percodan, I felt numb and warm and good, and it substantially lowered my stress. *What could be wrong with that*, I thought, *considering what we're going through?*

❋

Joan and I spent our days watching TV or videos I'd rented. I tried to find movies that were positive, uplifting, or funny—no high dramas. I had heard about Norman Cousins's books on how laughter aids healing, so I figured watching comedies might help. At least they'd distract her for a little while. We were trying anything that might help her heal. We even grew a kombucha mushroom—a health fad at the time—and she drank tea made from it that tasted weird and awful.

On the music front, not much was happening, other than Geffen gearing up to release our second single, "Ready For Love" (a song with a very catchy chorus, which years later, would be in contention to be recorded by Whitney Houston). I'd written the lyrics for it at Joan's (before she and I had gotten together) after Rachel and I had had a fight. Basically, it was about not wanting to say goodbye to a lover before giving the relationship one last chance. It had certainly been wishful thinking on my part.

Rachel and I were getting along fine, and we did some phone interviews now and then, but that was it for band business. We'd also started talking again about whether to officially come out. After all the press we'd done, we realized we had come across as fake and bubble-gummy. None of the edgier magazines wanted to profile us, because they knew we were gay but we wouldn't discuss it. *Rolling Stone* and *Vanity Fair* had told us they'd only interview us if we talked about our sexuality. Since we wouldn't, we were stuck doing stories for *Us, Playgirl*, and teenybopper magazines. *The Advocate* pitched us to come out in their pages, but we decided against it. Meanwhile, k.d. lang's album *Ingenue* was a huge hit, and she had come out. Ceremony had almost no following, and we'd done nothing to court the one group—lesbians—who would probably have supported us the most.

It would have helped if we had appeared the slightest taboo, because otherwise we seemed to be prefabricated crap. It was ironic: Our Geffen A&R person had worked with the blond-haired duo Nelson (Rick Nelson's twin sons), and we had thought we were the antithesis of such an appearance-conscious, sweet-pop teen group. Now we felt we *were* Nelson. Without planning it, Rachel's and my hairdos were the same, making us look like twins. We were dressing in a flashy way that didn't feel right, and our band had been created for us. We had begun this adventure thinking we were cutting-edge pop, but ended up just plain pop rock.

Rachel really wanted us to come out because she thought it would finally make us "real." Our manager Doc McGhee was pretty much in favor of it as well. Hiding our sexual orientation had required us to keep up a false front, and it had affected our songwriting and performances. I knew Rachel was right, and I knew there was nothing left to lose, career-wise. But I agreed with our publicist in thinking that if we came out at this point, it would be perceived only as an insincere attention-getting stunt.

Around this time we fired Doc McGhee, since he and his company didn't seem to be fighting for us. While our first single tanked, they watched it sink, telling us it was dead after only two weeks on the air. A lot of bands struggle, and it takes a while for a single to move up the charts, but good management continues to work for you. Instead, our management blamed the record company, never themselves.

At this point, Geffen Records wasn't much help either, but you can't fire your record company as easily as your manager. Initially the company had shown incredibly high expectations for our band, partly based on the music and partly on my notoriety. They thought we'd be a slam-dunk, like other contemporary "children of" bands—Nelson and Wilson Phillips—and they'd supported our recording with a large budget. But when we didn't immediately take off, it felt like Geffen Records decided, "Next!" They blamed all the problems on us, saying we weren't going that extra mile and weren't playing everywhere we could. We were caught, though, between a financial rock and a hard place, because our band members wanted to be paid for every gig and every rehearsal. They were only a band for hire, not invested in the group as our New York band had been. Before the single had come out and failed, Geffen Records had paid them. Now it was up to us, and we couldn't afford it.

We hired a new manager who was the founder and lead singer of a heavy metal band which was also on Geffen and A&R'd by John Kalodner. He started booking us some local gigs and setting up a California tour for us.

Kimberly, the gay Geffen Records promotion person who had befriended us in Chicago, tried to help us out by getting us a gig at the opening of a Bullocks department store in the Valley. We knew we were in big career trouble, reduced to playing at a department store. It could only have been worse if we were asked to play at the opening of a Marshalls.

All in all, things weren't going well. My career was falling to shit, my girlfriend was critically ill, and the responsibility for everything felt like it was on my shoulders. For a twenty-four-year-old, that's a very heavy load.

✳

As expected, the chemo once again caused Joan's blood counts to plummet. She was neutropenic and thus had to be readmitted to the hospital. Joan hated being there, but it was somewhat easier for me, although I was intensely bored there and drained from sleeping on the cot in Joan's room. I was still taking Percodan. I didn't get so high on it that I couldn't do everything I needed to for Joan, but it definitely made sitting around at the hospital more pleasant. I'd become completely desensitized to the hospital environment—it was almost funny remembering how disturbed I'd felt the first few times I walked down the halls and saw all the sick people in their rooms. It didn't affect me at all now.

Toward the end of Joan's ten-day stay, we received some heartening news: She was finally in remission. Now there was real hope that this might work. The chemo the doctors were now using on her would be part of the cocktail used for the stem-cell transplant, so knowing that it had been effective made us believe the stem-cell transplant might actually cure her cancer.

Now it was time for the stem-cell harvesting, which required several three-to-five-hour sessions in a special blood donor room that held the large equipment that was required. It wasn't a painful procedure, but Joan had to lie in a bed for hours, tubes running in and out of her. During one of the sessions, she didn't feel well, so I comforted her while sitting on the edge of her bed, holding her hand and stroking her arm—nothing a person wouldn't do for a friend or family member. But a female doctor on duty came over and told me, "This is a public place. You can't do that type of behavior here."

Amazingly, I did what she asked and moved away from Joan. When I thought about my response later, I was appalled. I couldn't believe I didn't tell her to go fuck herself. But I was in an altered state. And still in the closet.

The hospital stay was otherwise uneventful, and all of Joan's vital signs improved: Her blood counts climbed back up, and a CAT scan and bone marrow biopsy affirmed that she was in remission. Systems were "go" for the next stage, during which she'd receive the chemo and then the stem cells. It was mid December, and we'd be going home for a week before returning for the transplant.

We were still quite optimistic; Joan was feeling the best she had in months. During that week at home, she even got to see me perform with the band at Molly Malone's bar in Los Angeles. Joan loved watching me play onstage—it was a rock-star fantasy for her. She used to love when I'd sing or play for her at home too, telling me I was her sexy little rock star.

We made love again that week, though Joan was very sensitive about me getting too close to the Hickman, which was still embedded in her chest. She no longer felt comfortable with her body, which was a dramatic switch. She had always been very physically expressive and sexual. She had never been self-conscious—quite the opposite— but the illness and the chemo had taken a toll. Joan's voluptuous, well-toned body now seemed kind of shriveled, and I definitely saw the wear and tear on her face. For the first time, she looked her age.

We were hoping to postpone the stem-cell transplant until after Christmas, because we were miserable at the thought of spending the holiday season in the hospital, but the doctors insisted on carrying it out right away. I had hoped to take Joan to Aspen with me too, as I hadn't the Christmas before, because my family was now very comfortable with our relationship. I had even said to Joan last year, when I was so upset about leaving her, "Next year we'll be together in Aspen." Instead, not only would Joan be stuck in the hospital, but for only the second time in my life I wouldn't be with my family for the holidays. I couldn't leave her at a time like this.

Before we returned to Cedars, we at least got to attend a wonderful Christmas party—given by, of all people, Rachel. The relationship between Joan and Rachel had finally thawed, thanks to Rachel's kind efforts on Joan's behalf. Joan had required numerous transfusions of blood and platelets, and donating platelets takes a couple of hours. The tedious procedure is almost like stem-cell harvesting: The donor's blood is drawn out, run through a machine to remove the platelets, then reinfused in the donor's bloodstream. Rachel was generous enough with her time, and blood, to donate platelets, and that's when she and Joan had started talking again.

Rachel also visited and brought flowers to the hospital. She was the one to break the ice between them; I don't think Joan would have made the first move to patch things up. They didn't make any sort of formal amends or discuss anything with each other. They both just let go of the old feelings.

SEVEN

A day or so after Rachel's party, right before Christmas, Joan went back to Cedars to undergo the transplant. Depressed and tired, I didn't want to spend the holidays in the hospital, but I felt a certain amount of excitement too. Joan and I assumed the transplant would work, and this would be the start of her healing.

The first procedure she underwent was an operation to take some bone marrow from her hip, as a precaution in case the stem cells didn't do the job. Two days later the transplant began in a specially designated room on the fourth floor of Cedars, which had a sophisticated filtration system to protect patients from germs. Over the next several days, Joan's blood was infused with a cocktail of several types of chemotherapy designed to obliterate her bone marrow and all of her blood cells. The chemo was in such a large amount and so toxic that it would leave her blood counts at zero. Two days after her last chemo treatment, when the chemicals had left her body, she received the stem cells, which would then re-create her blood system—hopefully without cancer cells.

A peculiar and particularly awful side effect of the stem-cell infusion was the odor it produced. The cells were stored in a solution that smelled like a combination of sulfur and garlic, and after they were injected into Joan's bloodstream she would breathe the odor out. She didn't have ordinary bad breath—the stench in her room was so strong that it could be smelled down the hospital hallway and lingered for days. I couldn't get too close to her because it was so awful, but she couldn't smell it at all. The whole situation became a bit comical, as everyone reacted to the odor as soon as they entered the room.

When I wasn't with Joan in the hospital, I was Christmas shopping for both of us at the Beverly Center, the large mall across the street. She wanted a Christmas tree but wasn't allowed to have a real one in her room, so I bought her an artificial one, which we then decorated with white lights and ornaments from her collection. Even with its brightness, the tree didn't create much of a cheery mood.

It was incredibly disheartening to greet Christmas morning in a hospital room. Friends stopped by with presents, cookies, and candy, but since restaurants were closed I ended up eating Christmas dinner in the hospital cafeteria.

As my present to her, I gave Joan a platinum-and-diamond ring from her favorite designer, Pepe. Her gift to me was a Motorola pager. The device had just come out and seemed really cool, but to me it symbolized a stark change in our relationship, and a change in Joan herself. She had always been such a free spirit, but now she depended on me for absolutely everything. The pager symbolized her need to be in touch with me at any moment, so that I could fulfill her ever more desperate needs. That was uncharacteristic of Joan—in the past she would never have wanted to be bothered by a pager, or have needed to know where I was at all times. It was the last thing I wanted from her.

As sick as Joan had been before the transplant, nothing prepared us for the side effects she was now experiencing from the heavy doses of chemo. She developed many sores in her mouth, which spread down her esophagus and into her intestines, making it too painful for her to swallow food. She had to be put on an IV diet. Tiny rash-like hemorrhages broke out all over her body, caused by a lack of platelets needed to coagulate her blood. On top of that, Joan experienced some loss of control over her bowels and developed terrible hemorrhoids, for which she had to take sitz baths.

The chemotherapy also induced a temporary dementia, magnified by the large quantities of pain medication Joan was taking. She was lucid some of the time, but often she didn't make sense at all. Then again, it was probably good that she was in a sort of delirious state, because later she wouldn't remember the pain and humiliation. By now Joan didn't seem to care about much of anything. She wouldn't even put on the little brimless cap she'd worn since she had first lost her hair. She'd become too sick to care about what had always been so important to her: her appearance.

With Joan often incoherent, I felt more alone than ever at the hospital. At least I could talk to her before this; now I was left on my own to worry about her declining blood count and whether the stem-cell transplant was working. The drop in her blood count was expected but still scary, especially considering her previous post-chemo infection. She was much sicker now, so I was concerned that if she contracted an infection it would have far more devastating consequences. The fact is, most people who die from a stem-cell transplant do so when they acquire an infection that can't be controlled.

Even though I now had the pager she gave me, Joan became irrationally upset every time I planned to leave the hospital. The woman who had always encouraged me to do things for myself had turned into a sickly, terrified, insecure, completely dependent person. I was still in love with her, no question about that, but after the transplant I talked to Rachel about whether I'd ever be able to forget what Joan and I had gone through. I had so many dark and difficult images of Joan in my mind— Joan with sores everywhere, urinating and defecating on herself, acting crazy. Would I be able to get past these memories after she was well? I didn't know whether she'd ever be able to return to the full-of-life person she was, and if she did I wasn't sure I'd be able to think of her in the same way I had.

On New Year's Eve, my friends were going out to dinner, then meeting afterward at Rachel's. I wanted to join them at midnight, just to say hello and have a glass of champagne. But Joan and I got into a huge argument over this. We had rarely fought before she'd gotten sick.

"How can you leave me alone on New Year's Eve?" she asked me, even after I reassured her that I wouldn't leave until she fell asleep. I told her I just wanted to go out and have a drink with my friends. I was so upset about this that I talked with the social worker on the ward, who suggested I go anyway, saying it was unfair of Joan to make such a request.

But I was still very submissive, afraid of incurring anyone's anger, so I ended up promising Joan I wouldn't go. Sure enough, she fell asleep by ten o'clock and didn't wake up at all during the night, because she was so out of it from all the pain and antianxiety meds and chemo-induced dementia.

✳

In the weeks after New Year's, Joan's blood counts slowly rose, and the chemo-induced side effects diminished. We were all relieved, because the rise in blood counts meant the stem cells were taking hold and growing. The doctors wanted Joan's counts higher, though, before she could leave the hospital.

What shook us up most that month—literally—was the Northridge earthquake, which hit at four-thirty A.M. on January 17th. Joan and I were both asleep in the hospital, and the quake was so strong—6.7 on the Richter scale—that it threw me off my cot. *We're going to die!* I thought, expecting the building to collapse. Luckily, Joan stayed securely in her bed and was no longer hooked up to IVs. If she had been, the IV pole would surely have fallen down and torn the Hickman out of her chest.

Everything was a mess around us: Car alarms were going off all over the city, broken glass from Christmas tree ornaments littered the floor of Joan's room, and the hospital was in disarray, operating on auxiliary power. We couldn't even find out what was happening until someone located a transistor radio.

The next few days were frightening, especially every time an aftershock hit. Cedars is built on rollers, like a lot of tall structures in Los Angeles, so each tremor made the building rock and roll for a very long time. My nerves were already shot, and this didn't help. But I was stuck there because Joan didn't want me to leave her. Everyone was afraid to travel much after the quake; no one came to visit or relieve me. And I didn't eat much for a couple of days, since the hospital cafeteria had shut down.

After the quake, when the city was starting to get back to normal, Rachel and I began to tiptoe out of the closet. Our band played for the opening of the Love Lounge, a Saturday-night lesbian club promoted by L.A.'s well-known Girl Bar. It was our first time playing to a totally lesbian audience and the place was packed, with a line of women down the block waiting to get in. We'd never played in front of this large an audience with our entire band, and it was the first time we'd acknowledged the lesbian community at all. But there had been a buzz about us in the community for a long time—ever since I was outed by the tabloids —and the women at the Love Lounge definitely knew who we were. Even if we weren't officially out, they knew we were gay.

While a standing-room crowd filled the club's dance floor and grooved to our beat, we played a set of ten songs, including a couple of covers so that people could hear something familiar. We did "Oh, Darling" by the Beatles, Ringo Starr's "It Don't Come Easy," and the Rolling Stones' "It's All Over Now." On the last song,

Rachel sang, "I used to run around / With every girl in town," and the audience went wild.

It was a conscious decision on our part, supported by both our management and record company, to play a lesbian club. We'd finally decided to tap into that audience and try to garner a following among gay women. We knew we'd made a big mistake by not coming out during our press tour, but we figured that if we started playing these sorts of gigs without making a big deal about it, we wouldn't be seen as coming out just for the sake of publicity.

Rachel and I loved playing to gay women (the guys in the band didn't mind either), both that night and a few months later at the annual Dinah Shore golf tournament in Palm Springs. I felt so much more at ease among the lesbian community: They were already on our side, so we didn't have to try to win them over. For the first time, I got the feeling that people were supporting us not just because of who my parents were, but because we were a talented, lesbian-fronted band.

✳

At the end of January, Joan was finally considered well enough to go home. I thought it was a little premature, which I told the doctors, because she still seemed so sick and her blood counts weren't as high as they'd been the last time she was sent home. But the doctors reassured me that she was ready. Considering the nature of stem-cell transplants, they expected it would take Joan six months to return to normal anyway, and they thought her going home would aid her recovery.

I took her back to the Valley and we settled in. At this point she looked emaciated; the sores in her mouth and digestive track had made it difficult for her to eat. She seemed to have aged ten years in the hospital. I just kept telling myself that this was temporary. The doctors said it would be a long, slow recovery but that she'd eventually be back to who she was.

Just a few days after Joan came home, our band set out on a short Northern California tour set up by our new manager. Unfortunately, all the money we earned would go toward paying the other players, because they wouldn't participate without a money guarantee. The only thing keeping me going financially was that my mom was sweet enough to give me $5,000 for Christmas that year. I got a lot less money from my parents than people would imagine; they didn't overindulge me like they easily could have.

The tour would only take me away for four days, and Amy offered to stay with Joan. Joan was still taking Dilaudid, Ativan, and medications to help regenerate her red and white blood cells, so I prefilled all the syringes she'd need and instructed Amy on what to give Joan and when.

We took a van out on the tour and actually had a great time. The fact that Rachel and I weren't making any money erased the "us versus them" barrier that had existed before. I was especially happy just to get out of the house and rest. Being on the road is exhausting for most performers, but I hadn't slept through an entire night in months, so to me it felt like a resort vacation.

Being with a bunch of rowdy guys also helped take my mind off things. We had two unsophisticated Southern roadies with us who were hilarious. We all cruised girls together, and when they'd make crude remarks, it would crack us up. Rachel and I felt like we were just two of the guys, and we enjoyed the group spirit.

Joan had been OK about my going on tour, because it was for work, but when I got home I immediately noticed how very sick she looked. Even in the short time I'd been away she seemed to have grown more ill. The remainder of her eyebrows and eyelashes had disappeared, due to the chemo, and it made her look odd. She tried to look nice for me, putting on one of her wigs and a little makeup and an outfit other than pajamas, but her efforts merely accentuated how thin and sick she looked.

In the next few days, Joan grew increasingly disoriented and confused. She slept most of the time, and when she woke up she'd still be out of it. "What time is it?" she'd ask, and when I'd answer "Three o'clock," she'd think I meant three in the morning. She was also having auditory hallucinations of different people coming to the house. Once she heard a lawn being mowed and thought it was Scotti's godson Christian riding his motorcycle in her yard.

Concerned, I called Barry, who asked to see Joan in his office the next day. He thought the cancer might have spread to her brain. This terrified and confused me. Joan had been in remission before she had started the transplant, so how could the cancer return and go to her brain during the stem-cell process? It didn't make sense.

Shortly after talking to Barry, I got a phone call from our manager, who'd just gotten off the phone with John Kalodner. Geffen Records had decided that instead of releasing our second single and spending more money on us, they were going to cut their losses and drop us from the label. They'd already pressed the single, so I didn't understand how this would save them much money. Rather, I strongly suspected there was another reason for their action: Earlier that week, my mom had filed a suit to have Geffen release her from her contract with them, because she was unhappy with the way they had promoted her records. It seemed more than a coincidence that Geffen now had decided to drop Ceremony.

I was so concerned about Joan that I didn't have time to get really upset about this turn of events. Not until some time later would the sudden end of my music career really hit me. When I called Rachel with the news, she was much more emotional about it, but she didn't express her feelings too strongly because of what I was going through with Joan.

That afternoon I had an appointment at Cedars to donate blood for Joan. It only took an hour, but when I returned home there was an ambulance in the driveway. I rushed in to discover that Joan had fallen and was having difficulty breathing. Scotti, who had been staying with her, had called the paramedics.

Joan had had breathing difficulties before, but always due to anxiety. I suggested to the paramedics that I give her a shot of the tranquilizer Ativan through the Hickman, and they let me. But it didn't help, so they decided to take Joan to a nearby hospital in the Valley, where they gave her a variety of tests to find out the source of her breathing trouble. They didn't come up with an answer, so after conferring with Barry they decided that as soon as Joan had stabilized they'd transfer her to the ICU at Cedars.

While she was still in the hospital in the Valley, Joan and I had a casual conversation. I can't remember what we talked about. I just know that it was the last real conversation we would ever have.

✳

I wasn't allowed to spend the night with Joan in the ICU, so I went home. The next morning, I went straightaway to Cedars. As soon as I got there, before I even went to Joan's room, I asked the nurses if I could call Barry. They found me a private room with a phone.

"Have you been able to figure out why Joan's so sick?" I asked him. "Did the cancer go to her brain?"

"No, no, it hasn't gone to her brain. She has pneumonia," he told me.

I sighed with relief. "Oh, just pneumonia."

"Chas, it's really serious," Barry said somberly. He started to add something, but I cut him off.

"What do you mean?"

"Because the transplant has compromised Joan's immune system so much, the pneumonia has really progressed. We've started her on a course of very strong antibiotics, but she's in a dangerous place right now."

"Barry, what are you saying? Are you saying she's going to die?"

"I'm saying she could. The next forty-eight hours are critical. It's like we're in a race to see whether the antibiotics will take hold before the pneumonia can kill her."

I almost dropped the phone when I heard that. "Oh, my God. Are you doing *everything* you can?"

"Of course we are," he said. "Let's just try to stay positive for now. We'll know more in the next twenty-four hours. If you need me for anything, have me emergency-paged, and I'll get back to you immediately. Try not to worry. I'll call you if there are any changes in her condition."

I hung up and went to the ICU to see Joan. She looked deathly ill, hooked up to various monitors and catheterized both front and back. She was in such a foggy state that she barely noticed when I sat down next to her. It was difficult for her to talk, especially through the oxygen mask she was wearing, so she answered questions with few words. I was surprisingly calm, even though I was shocked by what Barry had told me. I stuck to my unshakable belief that as long as there was a chance that Joan *could* live, she *would*.

I spent the day with her, holding her hand and stroking her soft skin. I talked to her about insubstantial things, trying to soothe her. She spoke just a few words here and there, and only if I asked a direct question.

Joan was supposed to sign documents to release the hospital to perform certain treatments, but she couldn't write her name. I even tried to hold her hand and help her sign, but the signature came out as a scribble, so Barry put a living will in her chart that gave me the power to make medical decisions for her.

As the day wore on, Joan grew increasingly restless and seemed to be in a lot of pain. I went to ask the nurse when her next Dilaudid shot would be but learned that Sheldon Goldstein—the same doctor who had told us so coldly that if the chemo didn't work nothing more could be done—had prescribed a decrease in her dosage. He thought the Dilaudid could be making her disoriented. That didn't make any sense, though: Joan had been on the same dose of Dilaudid for months and was physically addicted to it, so now she was feeling withdrawal symptoms as well as missing its pain relief. I called Barry right away, furious that Joan was in pain at a time like this. He said he didn't know anything about Sheldon's instructions and immediately restored her usual dosage, which calmed her down a little. But she remained restless. Barry suggested that she wasn't getting enough oxygen to her brain because of the pneumonia.

Joan and I had never discussed the possibility of her dying. Talking about it seemed like an admission of defeat. We had tried so damned hard to be totally positive all the time. In our magical, wishful thinking we believed that if we never entertained the idea that she could die, it wouldn't happen. The closest we ever came to broaching the subject was one casual conversation about how Joan felt about death in general. I got the sense that she wasn't afraid of dying, which relieved me. But she also said she felt she still had a lot of life left to live.

Exhausted, I went home from the hospital at about ten o'clock that night. At that point, I wanted *something* to happen so that Joan would no longer be in such a horrible state. I wanted her to get better. Or—I have to admit this—if she wasn't going to get better, I wanted her to die. She had been in so much pain for so long. At that moment I thought I'd be relieved by this, having no idea how wrong I was.

The next morning I arrived at the hospital at around nine, and when I got to Joan's room I saw that she was now in hand restraints. Incensed, I went to the nurses' station to find out what was going on. They told me that Joan had been agitated all night and kept pulling at the different tubes, particularly the catheter collecting her urine. The nurse said that if I sat with her, I could remove the restraints.

As I walked back to Joan's room I thought, *Why don't they just talk to her and tell her not to pull out the tubes?* But when I arrived at her bedside, I realized that her condition had gone further downhill. She was practically comatose and only mildly responsive. If her hand was free she automatically pulled at the catheter, trying to remove it. There was no way anyone could tell her what to do; she was almost like an infant. I had only one of her restraints removed, and I held that free hand in mine, making sure she wouldn't use it to pull out anything.

I was mostly alone with her that day, as none of her friends came to the hospital. Scotti couldn't bring herself to see Joan like this. My sister Christy, though, dropped by that afternoon and stayed a couple of hours. She tried to talk with Joan, but it was impossible to have any real communication with her.

We didn't want to discuss Joan's situation within her earshot, even if she couldn't really hear us, so we left briefly to get a cup of coffee in a hospital lounge. Seeing Joan in such a state shook Christy up, but I was still in deep denial. It was so obvious how critical her condition was, yet I remained calm and even optimistic, despite her deterioration. I had become numb to reality. I kept thinking that the antibiotics were going to take effect soon and that Joan would eventually emerge from this state.

When Christy and I returned about forty-five minutes later, Joan had a terrible black eye—a huge swollen purple bump at her eyebrow line. I immediately ran to the nearest nurses' station.

"What happened?!" I asked a nurse.

"I don't know what you're talking about," she answered, looking puzzled.

"Joan's eye is nearly swollen shut. Come with me to look at it."

"She must have banged her head against the railing," the nurse said after she followed me back to Joan's room. Even the restraints couldn't stop Joan from accidentally hurting herself.

"Well, she's obviously either agitated or in pain," I said, fuming. "Can't you give her something?"

"I'll have to call the doctor," said the nurse. The standard response.

"If he gives you any problem," I said, barely staying calm, "tell me and I'll talk to him myself."

No one was at fault, but I just wanted to blame someone, anyone. Seeing Joan like this was completely demoralizing. There was nothing left of the woman she once was. Her spirit, her positive attitude, and her beautiful appearance—this terrible, terrible disease had ravaged everything.

That evening, Rachel came by the hospital. She briefly visited Joan, then we went into the waiting room to talk. It was getting late, around ten P.M., and Rachel said to me, "Why don't you spend the night at my house instead of going all the way back to the Valley? Then you can get to the hospital earlier in the morning." Rachel had recently moved to West Hollywood, just a few minutes from Cedars. She later told me she wasn't really trying to ease my trip to and from the hospital; rather, she suspected Joan wouldn't make it through the night. Rachel didn't want me to be alone when I got the news.

At Rachel's house we stayed up and talked for a while. Amy was there too, staying for a couple of weeks before she moved to Nashville. Since she was in the second bedroom, I ended up sleeping in Rachel's bed with her. We didn't cuddle; we were just platonic friends now. Exhausted, I fell right to sleep.

Around two-thirty in the morning, the phone rang. I looked at the clock, saw the time, and thought, *Oh, fuck, this isn't good.* I had left Rachel's number with the hospital staff in case Joan had any problems during the night. The phone was right next to the bed, but in my haste I jumped out of bed and stood facing the nightstand as I frantically picked up the receiver.

"Hello?!" I said.

"Chas?"

"Yeah?"

"It's Shelley." Sheldon Goldstein, the doctor I least liked in Barry's office, was on duty that night. "I'm very sorry," he said. "Joan's gone."

As I heard his words, my legs gave out. It was like an overdramatic movie cliché, but it happened: I fell right to my knees, sobbing, with the phone still at my ear.

"Shortly after you left, at about midnight, Joan's breathing became even more labored, so we made the decision to intubate her and hook her up to a respirator," he continued. "Two hours after that, she went into cardiac arrest. We tried to resuscitate her, but our attempts were futile."

I was crying so hard I was unable to speak. Rachel took the phone and quickly ended the call. After she calmed me down a bit, I phoned my mom in Malibu, where my aunt and her husband (who was a security agent for my mom) were also staying. My mom and aunt

drove over right away. Amy started cleaning the house—
that was the only way she could deal with the news. I
phoned Scotti, Leslie, and Barry. Then my mom and aunt
arrived, and we stayed up the rest of the night, talking
and crying and remembering Joan.

❋

The day after Joan died I returned to her house with
Rachel and Amy. We spend the next three days there
preparing for the funeral, along with Scotti and some other
close friends of hers and Joan's. Joan never made out a formal will; she had only written out informal ones boarding
an airplane, because she was terrified of flying. She had also
never bought a cemetery plot or made funeral arrangements. The one thing she had made clear to me was that
she wanted Scotti to be the executor of her estate. I
absolutely wanted to honor that, because Scotti had been
such a large part of her life for nearly thirty years, and I
knew she would do right by Joan.

We were all concerned about Joan's family learning of
her death. Joan had nothing to do with them after she
moved out at age seventeen, except for one visit with her
mom when she was nineteen. Nonetheless, we believed
that if they found out she had died they would want her
estate. Joan didn't have a tremendous amount of valuable
things, but her early 1970s Mercedes was worth about
$30,000, and she did have some nice jewelry, clothing,
and artworks. So we decided to remove her valuables
from the house and store them next door at Scotti's.

I ended up inheriting the Mercedes, because Joan had
told Scotti and me that she wanted me to have it—as long

as I then sold it, because Joan thought I was a lousy driver. I also kept some sentimental items of Joan's: jewelry, pictures, books, clothes. My most treasured inheritance was her gold Hawaiian cross with a J in the middle, hung on a Cartier chain. She used to give it to me to wear for good luck when I was traveling. I never take it off.

Scotti involved me in all the decision-making about the funeral. We chose Forest Lawn in the Valley as the place for Joan to be buried, and Scotti let me choose the casket. I also selected the plot site, among some trees with a bench nearby. I picked out the clothes Joan would be buried in too—her favorite pair of jeans and a cream-colored sweater with an exposed lower back. On her feet she would wear her favorite pair of cowboy boots. I suggested we bury her with the teddy bear I had gotten her when she first went into the hospital and the angel pin she wore on her brimless hat.

Scotti chose a lovely metal plaque for her grave, with a flower design around the edge that looked like a lei. Aside from Joan's name and her birth and death dates, Scotti ordered one additional line: "Dancing in Heaven." Joan always loved to dance, whether at clubs or just doing sexy moves for me at home. Dancing was the only job Joan had ever held. If there's a heaven, Joan is certainly dancing up there.

I threw myself into funeral preparations; it was the only thing that could take my mind off how despondent I was. There were so many people to call. I had to meet with the priest from Forest Lawn who would officiate at the ceremony and tell him about Joan's life. I had to buy a black suit for the funeral because I didn't own anything appropriate. I certainly couldn't wear my rock-star leather pants and my jacket that looked like an upholstered couch from the '60s, although perhaps Joan would have gotten a kick out of that.

I gave the morticians one of Joan's wigs and photographs of her to show how she wore her makeup. I wanted to see her body before the funeral, but my mom talked me out of it. No matter how good they could make her look, she reminded me, Joan would still look dead, and that would be my final image of her. I already had an awful final image of Joan—pale as a ghost, sporting a black eye, completely bald, with an oxygen mask covering her face and tubes running in and out of her. I didn't want to remember her that way either, but my mom convinced me it would be even worse to see her frozen in death.

I continued to live at Joan's house during this time, my friends staying with me. I was taking Percodan even more often than before, and seriously contemplating the idea of giving myself a shot of Dilaudid. I was in so much emotional pain that I didn't want to feel anything. My life as I had known it was over. I had no career, no partner. Joan hadn't just been my lover—she'd been a constant in my life since my early teens. I couldn't believe she was gone, and gone with her were all the wonderful things she had meant to me.

*

Joan's funeral was beautiful, attended by a couple hundred people. The priest struck just the right tone and the chapel at Forest Lawn looked gorgeous, filled with Hawaiian flowers Scotty ordered. Placed right behind the coffin was a huge pastel portrait of Joan, painted by an artist friend of hers. It captured her with astonishing likeness. I just wished Joan were there, and not a portrait. I couldn't stop thinking about her being in the coffin.

Several of Joan's friends took the podium to talk about what she meant to them. I came up last to deliver a eulogy I had written with Rachel's help. Here's some of what I said:

> I was in love with Joan and everything her life stood for. Simply put, she was the very best person I have ever known. When I was a kid Joan treated me like an adult, and now that I am an adult, she often brought out the kid in me. She never let me take myself too seriously, which I have a tendency to do, because she always wanted to remind me that life could essentially be fun. As she always said, life is about the three f's—fun, food, and... I think you all know what the third f stands for. Joan never got bogged down or hung up by a lot of the trivial stuff that most of us get caught up in. Namely, pursuing a career. She often said to me, "How do people hold down a job? When do they have time to live?"
>
> It gives me such a warm feeling to see how many lives Joan touched. Whether you were her lover or her gardener, an acquaintance or a life-long friend, she had an uncanny ability to make everyone feel special. She was a friend to all, a teacher to most, and threw the best damn parties that ever were.... When you stepped into

her world, you left your troubles behind, and if you brought them with you, they were gently indulged until they were purged.

Everyone that she's touched will carry a piece of Joan with them, and in that way she's not gone from us at all. But God I miss her. In my eyes she was the most beautiful, sexy, loving, courageous woman that ever was...

Joan always said that a relationship requires four elements: timing, lighting, chemistry, and balance. Joan and I achieved those elements together, and I feel honored that I was her last love. You know, Joan and I fought a war together these last nine months, and we swore that if we made it through that, we'd never be apart. Well, J.L., in our own way, we made it. We'll never be apart. I'll love you, baby, till the end of time.

I made it through the eulogy without crying. Only when we walked up to the burial plot did I start to lose it. Seeing her put into the ground, with people shoveling dirt on top of her coffin, was too much for me to take. I didn't do anything crazy—I just cried—but something in my head cracked. It felt like too much grief to bear, and I thought I was going insane.

Right afterward there was a wake for Joan at a lesbian bar in the Valley, an old dive where Joan occasionally went. The owner offered the space to Scotti when she heard about Joan's passing. Joan had been well known in the lesbian community—she had been out and about with Scotti since she was eighteen, and with her great looks she was always noticed. Until the days of "lesbian chic" in the mid 1980s, you wouldn't often see such an attractive, feminine woman as Joan in a cheesy gay bar. I'm sure that when this tall, voluptuous blonde with the killer body walked into a bar in her younger days, every head turned her way. Even when I was hanging out with her twenty years later, she turned at least two-thirds of the heads in a room. She always made a statement, just by her stunning appearance.

She was also such a friendly person, treating everyone she met with respect and sincerity. As I said in the eulogy, Joan had a gift for making anyone she talked to feel listened to and cared about. That's what people told me over and over again at the wake, even those who had only met her at a party or come over to her house once or twice. Yet they attended her funeral because she had touched their lives.

Even as I listened to their kind words, I wasn't feeling very present. I was detached, unable to connect with anyone. People kept coming up to me and giving their condolences, and I could barely cope. I left after only about forty-five minutes, along with Rachel, Amy, and our friend Doug.

Back at Joan's house, I popped some Percodan and slept for a while. I just wanted to isolate myself in my room. But my friends encouraged me to get up and be with them that evening. Doug, who had gone to high school with Rachel, had something else in mind. He knew about all the drugs I still had in the house and asked if I'd give him a shot of Dilaudid. I said yes.

Rachel, who had cleaned up her act, tried to talk us out of it. "You guys are acting crazy!" she said.

"Oh, Rachel, you're just being square," I responded. "Because you're sober now, you're trying to kill our fun."

I was feeling incredibly self-destructive, even suicidal—I'd been thinking and talking about killing myself—and I wanted to shoot up the Dilaudid myself. There was enough in the house to keep me from feeling any pain for *months*. But I was scared to inject myself. I needed a guinea pig, and Doug was perfect. I'd become so accustomed to caring for Joan by giving her shots that the thought of giving someone else a shot was comforting in a very twisted way. It reminded me of being Joan's caregiver, bringing me closer to her memory for a moment.

So I gave Doug a low-dose shot of Dilaudid in his arm. I didn't think it would cause any problems. The next morning, though, he had a seizure. Rachel came screaming to get me, and we called the paramedics. Strangely enough, I was hardly fazed by any of this. While Rachel panicked, I thought, *Whatever.* After all I'd been through with Joan, a little seizure seemed like no big deal. Plus, I was so wrapped up in my own pain that I'd become indifferent to that of others.

Thankfully, Doug came out of the seizure quickly. It turned out that he had taken a number of other drugs besides the Dilaudid, along with alcohol. I don't think he even told the paramedics that he'd been given Dilaudid. I'd been so stupid, though: I hadn't even thought of the legal ramifications when I gave him the injection. If it had killed or incapacitated him, I would have been criminally liable.

Rachel reminded me of this as we went to the hospital to see Doug. That's when I finally started to realize what I'd done. I especially worried about what my mom would think. I had always tried to be so responsible and straight-laced; I'd be mortified if my mom found out.

When we returned to the house, Rachel became great-ly concerned about me. She wanted me to give her the drugs that were still in the house, but I wouldn't. I locked myself in the bedroom where the drugs were kept, so Rachel called my mom and told her what was happening. She knocked on my bedroom door to say that my mom was on her way over.

I really lost it then. I stomped out of the house, because I didn't want to be there when my mom showed up. When Rachel came after me I balled my hand up into a fist and almost punched her. I kept walking, not know-ing where I was going. I just couldn't face my mom. But Rachel followed and finally talked a little sense into me.

"Where are you going? What are you going to do? Your mom's not mad at you—she's just *worried* about you."

By the time my mom showed up, along with my aunt and uncle, I had returned to the house. But I copped an attitude with them.

"I don't know what you're doing here, I don't know why Rachel called you," I said. "I'm fine, everything's fine."

As usual, my mom stayed cool and didn't get upset.

"It doesn't seem like you're fine, and I think you should come home for a while," she said in a caring voice. "Let me help you."

I realized she was right. Rachel and I went to her house, and I spent the next few days in bed, crying uncontrollably. That was really unusual for me, because I hate to cry. I've always looked at it as a sign of weakness. Even a few years later, when I found out that my dad had died, I didn't cry. But for those few days at my mom's house, I couldn't control myself. Even when I left the house for a short while, I carried a box of tissues because I was constantly breaking out in hysterical tears.

My mom suggested I see a therapist and got a few recommendations for me. I found someone whom I still occasionally visit. She helped me center myself again, and then I felt ready to return to Joan's. But that's when my mom received a call from Scotti. Scotti had decided to sell Joan's house right away, so she wanted to fix it up. She owned it, after all. Bottom line, she didn't want me to come back and live there. She didn't harbor any bad feelings toward me—this was just how she was dealing with her grief. For Scotti, losing Joan had been like losing a child, best friend, partner, and confidante. She wanted to get rid of the house, and all those memories, as soon as possible.

I felt hurt and angry, but part of me knew I couldn't go back and live there without Joan. It would only make me feel worse than I already did.

Epilogue

After Joan died, I saw Scotti only a few more times. My anger about being asked to leave the house had worn off, but we didn't stay close. About three years later, after having not spoken to her in nearly a year, my mom got a call from Scotti's brother saying she had died. She too had gotten cancer and, without telling anyone she was sick, had left Los Angeles to live—and then die—at her brother's. She was about seventy years old. It made sense to me that she passed away so soon after Joan, because she'd lived vicariously through her for so many years. I couldn't imagine Scotti being able to exist very well without Joan around; the pain was probably overwhelming for her. They were like an old married couple, where one goes and the other follows not long after.

I stayed with Rachel for a couple of weeks after I left my mom's, until I found an apartment near Rachel's in West Hollywood. I used to think that when a loved one dies, the most trauma you feel is right afterward, and then it decreases. But that's not how I experienced the loss of Joan. I just continued to sink further and further emotionally.

I tried to cover up my loss with other relationships, but that didn't work, and they didn't work out. When the next relationship I got involved in ended, my mourning wasn't really for that woman, but for Joan. Even when my dad died in 1998, I was in grief about Joan all over again. Then I got into another difficult relationship, trying to cover up the accumulated pain. The more I was unable to distract myself from the underlying feelings, the more life continued to disappoint me. Since I couldn't re-create what I'd had with Joan, her absence became excruciating.

I don't know where drug use fell into all that, except that I kept trying to stop the pain any way I could—whether it was with the wrong lovers or with prescription painkillers. Drugs are a quick fix. They work at first, but the sad truth is that they soon stop working and then create new problems to recover from. It wasn't until I stopped trying to avoid the pain that I started healing. But that's a story for my next book.

After Joan died, I briefly considered becoming a nurse. I craved taking care of someone, as I'd taken care of Joan. It would take me a good year to get past that feeling of wanting to be a caretaker. It's weird: You live a so-called normal life, then you find yourself in an abnormal, surreal experience, which over time becomes your normality. When the surreal experience ends, it leaves a void and you miss it. As hard as it had been taking care of Joan, the experience gave me a real sense of purpose and accomplishment. I didn't know what to do with myself after she was gone and I had no one to care for.

Fortunately, I did begin to find real passion and intensity again, but this time in my work rather than my love life. The record business was over for me, but I threw myself into journalism, writing for *The Advocate*, and became an activist for the gay and lesbian community. GLAAD hired me as their entertainment media director, and I wrote a successful book, *Family Outing*. I thought those achievements would finally give me credibility and an identity separate from that of my parents. I became extremely career-driven, looking to my work to give me the kind of fulfillment I wasn't finding personally.

Having people admire and respect me, consider me intelligent and interesting—the kinds of responses I received for what I was doing professionally—worked really well for a while. The praise made me feel great about myself. But then, like the drugs, it stopped working. I began to learn that you can't attain what you're looking for as a human simply from being admired by the public or becoming a financial success. Those things don't fill the hole inside. If you've never been taught how to be happy, it's hard to know how to achieve it. I've had to learn the hard way, getting knocked around by life.

I feel incredibly fortunate to have found Joan, because she did make me feel happy. She was unconditionally loving and nurturing, safe and consistent. We got something from each other that no one before had been able to give us: We were both loved and accepted in a devoted, uncomplicated way. We just wanted to please each other and take pleasure in each other. She relished taking care of me while she was well, and I didn't think anyone else could have done a better job caring for her when she became ill. It doesn't seem like a mistake or coincidence that, after everything we had been through for so many years, I was her last love.

Although Joan doesn't fill my waking thoughts as much as she did in the first years after her death, it's amazing how often I've dreamed about her. The first year she was gone I would dream that she was still alive—rather, that she had come back to life—but that she was still sick and wanted me to take care of her. I wanted to move on, though, and in my dreams I tried to negotiate the process with her. I guess a therapist would find that easy to interpret. I had missed out on a normal life for a time, so I was trying to make up for it. I didn't want to have to keep taking care of Joan; I wanted to make a *new* relationship work.

For the next couple of years, I dreamed that Joan was alive and healthy but that I was with someone else. I'd go back and forth in my dreams about whether I should be with Joan or stay with my current lover. Joan usually won out. Those dreams would correspond with times when my relationship wasn't going well. At least in my dreams I could always go back to Joan. During one particularly bad period, I dreamed that Joan had faked her death and was really alive but for some reason had cut me out of her life.

In the two years before I got clean of drugs, I thought of Joan constantly. Constantly! Then, after I did get clean, the dreams stopped for about nine or ten months.

That also corresponded with the time I met Stasie, my current girlfriend. I finally found myself in a very happy relationship—the best relationship I've been in, and the best emotional place I've been in, since Joan's death. I fell in love with Stasie because of the person she is, not because I was desperate to be in a relationship to temporarily smother my pain.

Recently I started to dream of Joan again, but the dreams are less formed. I just feel a closeness to her, although the details are vague. Joan sometimes feels *too* close. I want to be able to evoke her memory without it stopping me in my tracks. Even when she takes my attention for a long moment these days, I don't feel as much pain.

✳

My original reason for wanting to write about Joan was to keep living the experience I had with her. I wanted to be with her again. Now that I'm in a healthier place, I've been able to look back on her more objectively. There was an innocence and ease to our relationship that I'll never have again, because you can't get innocence back once it's lost. I was very young then, and Joan satisfied all my needs. Nobody could do that now and nobody should. Thinking about Joan again, I ended up writing as much about me as about her.

In fact, once I got clean, I didn't want to write about Joan at all. I wanted to work toward the future instead of living in the pain and loss of the past. The idea of going back through everything in such detail didn't seem pleasant at all. I finally wasn't hurting, so I was afraid of running back to the place that had been a source of agony for so many years. I was afraid of dwelling on the past, afraid I couldn't write about it without reliving it.

I'd be lying if I said it hasn't been hard dredging up some of the memories, but it's also helped me acknowledge that there was a reason I felt so traumatized afterward. Joan's illness and death were utterly cruel and shocking. It makes sense to me now why it messed me up to go through such an experience in my early twenties. I now know that it was OK that I let my life fall apart, because the pain was really too hard to bear at the time. I didn't have any tools to deal with it. Fortunately, now I've started to gather some of those tools.

I've never imagined what would have happened if Joan had never gotten sick. I *have* imagined what would have happened if she hadn't died. Actually, it scares me to think of whether our relationship would have worked in the long run as well as it did when we were together. The strange thing about death is that there's really no closure; everything just stops. You haven't broken up a relationship that has deteriorated. When Joan died, I was still madly in love with her, and that never went away. I've just finally been able to really love someone else too. It's funny, but the hardest parts of this book to write were about the good times I had with Joan, not the misery of her illness. When I remember the happiness we had, the friendship she gave me for so many years, I miss her so very, very much.

I think Joan would have absolutely adored having a book written about her. She would have loved being immortalized. To me, Joan always seemed too special of a person to be remembered only by her immediate friends.

In one recent dream that I recall, I'm at Joan's house, though she no longer lives there. I go into the house and tell the new residents about the woman who lived there before them. In other words, in my dream I did exactly what I'm doing in this book. Now a lot more people won't forget you, J.L.

Acknowledgments

I'd like to thank: Stasie Kardashian, for her constant love, support, and insights; Stinky Butt, for her love, warmth, inspiration, and stinkiosity; my mom, just for being who she is and for loving this book; Amy Ruskin, for her lifelong friendship and discretion; Dr. Barry Rosenbloom, for everything he's done and for being more than just a doctor; Sherry Lewis, for maintaining my sanity and giving me unconditional love and support; Loretta Barrett, for being the greatest agent on the planet and always watching my back; Jane Pasanen, for all her hard work and her help in setting up signings; Michele Kort, for helping me finally put the past in its place; Judy Wieder, for her love, undying support, and vision; and Angela Brown, for her pain-free edits and creative talents. —*C.B.*

First and foremost, thanks to Chas for entrusting me with her words and memories. It's been a pleasure collaborating with you. Big thanks to Judy Wieder of *The Advocate* for suggesting me for this project, to my agent Ellen Geiger for her wisdom and support, and to Angela Brown of Alyson for her excellent editing. Finally, thanks to everybody else who's been on my side, especially Miriam, Paula, my sister Melissa, my dad, and my wonderful aunts and uncles and cousins—and special shouts out to Stasie and to my furless co-cowriter, Ms. S.B. —*M.K.*